The Ultimate
Vegetarian
Cookbook

THE ULTIMATE
VEGETARIAN
COOKBOOK

ANNESS
PUBLISHING

Produced by Anness Publishing Ltd

ISBN 0-8317-9064-4

Reprinted in 1995

Publisher: Joanna Lorenz
Project Editor: Samantha Gray
Designer: Adrian Morris
Photographer: Michael Michaels
Home Economist: Wendy Lee

Printed and bound in China

 THE LEAF SYMBOL NEXT TO A RECIPE INDICATES THAT IT IS SUITABLE FOR VEGANS.

Please note that mushroom ketchup may be used as a vegetarian substitute for Worcestershire sauce.
Anchovy essence may also be omitted from recipes.

CONTENTS

INTRODUCTION

The fabulous range of healthy and delicious ingredients available today ensures that there are limitless possibilities for meat-free meals. Here you will find mouthwatering recipes for every occasion.

Introduction

The human body needs certain nutrients if it is to remain in perfect working order, to be fully effective, and alert, to keep energy levels high and resistance to illness strong, to help young bodies grow and for older bodies to get the most from life.

The human being is naturally omnivorous, in that the body can digest a wide range of foods, but it also has a discerning and intelligent brain which enables it to make different choices. For an increasing number of people in the Western world, the choice is being made to eat flesh-free meals, consuming foods that do not contain animal products or cause animals suffering or death.

The growth of vegetarianism in the West, through choice rather than necessity or religious beliefs, has focused our attention on the tremendous attractiveness of meat-free dishes. We have discovered the joy of cooking with foods such as grains, pulses and vegetables. We begin to appreciate the sheer beauty of the colors, shapes and textures of these foods. It has made many of us look again at our diets and methods of cooking.

So, this book is written not just for those converted to the virtues of vegetarianism, but is also intended to tempt 'omnivores' to the vegetarian way of eating and to show that it is possible to produce a delicious and attractive meal,

free from the tyranny of the 'meat and two veg' way of menu planning.

The ideal well-balanced diet is one that contains sufficient levels of calories, proteins, carbohydrates, fats, vitamins and minerals. No one food contains all the nutrients we need, although some contain more than others and some vitamins can only be obtained easily through animal products. The secret for eating a well-balanced, healthy diet is to eat a wide variety of foods to ensure you include all the nutrients you need. A few likes and dislikes may not cause problems, but too many fads may mean you are not taking all the nutrients your body needs.

So the golden rule that nutritionists and doctors ask us to practice is to eat all foods in moderation and to eat a great variety of foods. This variety is especially important for vegetarians; the occasional indulgence is fine, but too much of one or two foodstuffs (especially fats) could cause health problems.

Because vegetarians eat more grains, vegetables, pulses and fruit in their diet than meat eaters, they seem to obtain a greater amount of dietary fiber, or as it is now known NSP (non-starch polysaccharides). However, they have to

be careful not to increase their intake of high fat dairy products such as cheese, butter and cream. Just like meat eaters, they should watch their intake of these potentially high cholesterol products. Where possible choose lower fat versions. There are an increasing number on the market which are usually well labeled. Changing from full fat milk to skim or semi-skim milk helps, as does eating plenty of low fat yogurts, cottage cheese and skim milk soft cheeses.

Iron can also be a particular problem for vegetarians if they are not aware of the sources from which it can be obtained. Also, iron from vegetable sources cannot be utilized by the body unless there is vitamin C present in the same meal to act as a catalyst. But a small piece of fruit, fresh salad or even a good squeeze of lemon juice soon redresses that problem.

Vegans (those who exclude dairy products from their diet) need to ensure they take in sufficient calcium either in the form of calcium tablets or calcium enriched soya milk. They may also need to supplement their diet with other vitamins such as Vitamin B2 (riboflavin) and B12 and minerals such as iodine, which can be obtained simply by using iodized salt. A vegan diet can be just as healthy as a well-balanced omnivorous diet, so long as followers are well informed about suitable foods.

AIM TO EAT EACH DAY

A GOOD SELECTION FROM EACH

OF THESE CATEGORIES

☐ Grains, including pasta, rice (brown and white), oats (including porridge), barley, quinoa and high fiber breakfast cereals or crackers

☐ Breads and potatoes, cooked with the minimum of oil, butter or cream

☐ Pulses and legumes such as lentils, kidney beans, split peas, aduki beans etc.

☐ Plenty of fresh vegetables, especially leafy greens such as spinach, and fresh fruits

☐ Low fat natural/unsweetened yogurt, skim milk cottage cheese or low fat ricotta

☐ Moderate amounts of dried fruits (apricots, prunes, raisins etc.) and

unsalted nuts (peanuts, almonds, walnuts, hazelnuts etc.)

☐ Cautious amounts of cheese, especially high fat types

☐ Cautious amounts of oils, margarines, butter and cream

☐ Occasional cautious amounts of processed foods with high 'hidden fats' such as cookies, cakes, potato chips and pastries

THE VEGETARIAN PANTRY

The starchy foods

Nutritionists and doctors are now encouraging us all to eat a great deal more of complex carbohydrate foods, which is great news for vegetarians and all creative cooks, as these foodstuffs are all so versatile, nourishing and – best of all – cheap. They also store well without refrigeration and can be cooked with the minimum of preparation. Starchy foods have reasonable amounts of protein plus vitamins from the B group and minerals such as phosphorous, zinc, iron, potassium and, in the case of bread, added calcium. The other main advantage is they are good sources of dietary fiber (NSP).

Flours

Have a selection of different flours to add variety. Often it is a good idea to mix two types together in baking for flavor and texture. Use half whole wheat and half plain white flours for a lighter brown pastry crust or bread loaf. Mix buckwheat flour with plain white for pancakes and so on. Flour is a good source of protein as well as complex starchy carbohydrate, and indispensable in cooking. If you don't buy flour often, buy it in small amounts and store in an airtight container.

Brown/whole wheat flours and buckwheat have a shorter shelf life than the more refined white flours. Remember too, that self-rising flours with their added rising agent lose their lightening ability after about six months.

Rice

There is an increasingly attractive range to choose from. Ideally, avoid easy-cook rice as this has a chewy texture and much of the natural flavor processed out of it. The pre-steaming process does mean, however, that marginally more of the water soluble vitamins and minerals are retained.

Top of the rice range is basmati, an elegant, fragrant, long grain rice grown in the foothills of the Himalayas. Traditionally eaten with curries, basmati is marvelous in almost all dishes, sweet and savory, especially pilafs. Brown basmati is a lighter wholegrain rice with higher levels of dietary fiber. Thai rices are delicate and lightly sticky and are particularly good in stir-fries and wonderful in milk puddings. Wild rice (not a real rice, but an aquatic grass) has good levels of proteins. Pre-soaking shortens the cooking time.

Pasta

The mainstay of many a cook in a hurry. Again, a good source of starchy complex carbohydrates. Available in a multitude of shapes, colors and now even flavors. Good pasta should cook to a tender texture but retain a firm bite, which the Italians call *al dente* (to the tooth). For this, choose pasta that is made with durum wheat or durum semolina. Cook pasta in plenty of boiling salted water according to the instructions on the package, then drain it, rinse well in cold running water and shake lightly. Italians tend to serve pasta slightly wet. Return to the pan with some olive oil, seasoning and a grating of fresh nutmeg.

Whole wheat pastas have a more nutty flavor and chewy texture. They are particularly good in creamy sauces such as macaroni and cheese. Choose pasta shapes to match the sauce. Long thin pasta such as linguine and spaghetti are best served with light thin sauces; shells and tubes are complemented well by creamy and rich sauces.

Potatoes

Like rice, potatoes are beginning to enjoy something of a culinary renaissance as more cooks realize that choosing the right variety for a dish is one secret of success. Also, more potatoes are being grown for flavor and are often delicious served simply boiled in their skins lightly dressed with a little olive oil or butter. Choose small waxy firm potatoes for salads, larger firm ones for roasting, and floury varieties for mashing. More and more producers are printing suitable uses on the bags, so check these first.

Pulses

Over half the world's main source of protein comes from pulses in one form or another. However, although high in protein, pulses are not complete in all amino acids. In particular they lack one of the amino acids called methionine. Grain foods on the other hand lack lysine and tryotophan, which pulses do have. But, put them together and you have completed the usual protein circle. So, when you eat any pulses try to include starches in the same meal, such as lentils with rice, humus with bread, beans with pasta and so on. In addition include some fresh vitamin C in the meal (from fruits or leafy vegetables) so that your body can utilize the iron in the grains and pulses.

The variety of pulses is exciting and seemingly endless. Dried pulses benefit from soaking, preferably overnight. Older pulses may need longer. To shorten soaking time, cover with boiling water and leave for 2 hours. Drain and boil in fresh water. Boil pulses fast for the first 10 minutes of cooking to destroy any potential mild toxins present. Then lower the heat and gently simmer. Do not add salt or lemon juice during cooking as this toughens the skins, although fresh herbs and onion slices add flavor. Like pasta, don't overdrain. Leave wet. Season and maybe dress with extra virgin olive oil.

Certain lentils can be cooked without pre-soaking. The small split red lentils (or Masoor Dhal) are marvelous for sprinkling in as thickeners for soups and stews and take just 20 minutes to cook. Beans with a good creamy texture that is perfect for soups, patés and purées are butter beans, kidney beans (red and black), cannellini, navy, borlotti, pinto beans and flageolets. Split peas and red lentils make marvellous dips. Chick peas and aduki beans hold their texture well during cooking and make a good base for burgers and stews.

Fats and oils

For general frying, choose oils high in polyunsaturates. Sunflower, rape seed and groundnut have the lightest flavors and these are the ones preferred by gourmet cooks. Corn oil and blended vegetable oils are stronger in flavor. Increasingly popular is olive oil. Not only highly prized for flavor, it also has properties beneficial to health, being high in monosaturates which are thought to help reduce blood cholesterol levels. Two main qualities are available – pure olive oil, excellent for general cooking, and extra virgin oil made from the first cold pressing of the olives, producing a full-flavored, almost peppery taste, ideal for dressing salads and as a healthier flavor substitute for butter. Aromatic seed and nut oils (e.g. sesame, walnut and hazelnut) are too heavy and expensive for general use, but they are ideal for trickling on hot vegetables, pulses or pasta. Store these aromatic oils in the fridge. Others are fine kept at room temperature.

All fats, unless labelled specifically 'lower' or 'reduced fat' contain approximately the same amount of calories. It is the type of fat within them that counts healthwise. Sunflower and olive oil spreads are lower in harmful saturates and higher in healthier polyunsaturates and monosaturates. Spreads labelled 'low fat' or 'reduced fat' will have more added water which helps reduce the calories, but also makes them more difficult for frying and baking.

Fats and oils are important in our diets, contributing vital vitamins such as A, D and E, so do not cut them out altogether. Include them in moderate amounts. Check package labels for full nutritional details and remember to restrict your fat intake to no more than a third of your total daily intake of calories.

Cheese

A popular high protein food with vegetarians, cheese is also high in calories, having twice the number of many carbohydrate and protein foods. For fuller flavor choose well aged varieties of cheese such as a sharp farmhouse Cheddar or fresh Parmesan – you will then not need to use as much.

Many vegetarians seek out cheeses made with vegetarian rennet and more of the popular cheeses are made this way.

For cooking, choose aged cheeses. I like to leave some full flavored cheeses unwrapped in the refrigerator to dry out – this concentrates the flavor and makes them go further when finely grated.

Lower fat cheeses are often not as full flavored as normal varieties and the temptation is to use more of them, which rather counteracts their purpose!

My favorite cheeses include sharp Cheddar, fresh Parmesan, aged Gruyère and Pecorino – an Italian sheep cheese. Lower fat soft cheeses and goat cheeses are ideal for stirring into hot food to make an instant tasty, creamy sauce.

Dairy products

Supermarket dairy sections carry a great range of cultured dairy goods which present many exciting opportunities for the home cook. Crème frâiche is a French-style sour cream which does not curdle when boiled, so it is ideal stirred into hot dishes. It will also whip, adding a light piquancy to desserts. However, like heavy cream it is quite high in fat – 40% – so use it sparingly.

Low fat ricotta is a smooth, lightly tangy, lower fat to virtually fat-free creamy cheese ideal for use in dressings, baked potatoes and desserts. Quark is a soft cheese made with skim milk and so is very low in fat. It can be used in cheesecakes instead of cream cheese, but it is ideal for savory dishes too. Cream and cottage cheeses are long time favorites, and both are now available in very low fat versions too for healthier eating.

Be sure to check all cheese labels first if you are looking for those made with vegetable rennet.

Dairy-free products

The unassuming soy bean is one of the best sources of high vegetable protein foods. As such, it is ideal as a base for dairy-free milks, creams, fat spreads, ice creams and cheeses, making it perfect for vegans and those with dairy product allergies. Use these products in the same way as their dairy counterparts, although those changing over will find that the soy products taste slightly sweeter.

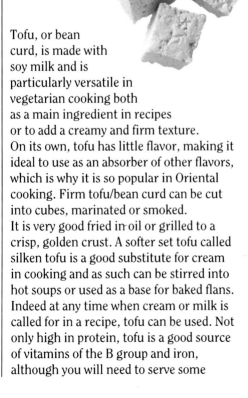

Tofu, or bean curd, is made with soy milk and is particularly versatile in vegetarian cooking both as a main ingredient in recipes or to add a creamy and firm texture. On its own, tofu has little flavor, making it ideal to use as an absorber of other flavors, which is why it is so popular in Oriental cooking. Firm tofu/bean curd can be cut into cubes, marinated or smoked. It is very good fried in oil or grilled to a crisp, golden crust. A softer set tofu called silken tofu is a good substitute for cream in cooking and as such can be stirred into hot soups or used as a base for baked flans. Indeed at any time when cream or milk is called for in a recipe, tofu can be used. Not only high in protein, tofu is a good source of vitamins of the B group and iron, although you will need to serve some vitamin C at the same meal to utilize it as a vegetable source of iron.

Mycoprotein (sold under the brand name Quorn), is a new man-made food which is a distant relation to the mushroom. Low in fat and calories, it is high in protein with as much fiber as green vegetables. It cooks quickly, absorbing flavors as easily as bean curd, and has a firmer texture. It is good for stir-frying, stews and casseroles.

Nuts and seeds

Not only full of flavor, texture and color, nuts and seeds are great nutritional power packs. But like cheese, they can be high in fats as well as proteins, so go easy.

Cheapest and most versatile are peanuts which are best bought unsalted or even better, roasted unsalted. Almonds (blanched or in flakes) are also very useful as are walnuts, pine nuts, hazelnuts and the more expensive cashews. Often it is nice to mix two or three together. But nuts can go rancid if stored too long (over six months or so), so if you are not a regular user, buy in small amounts. Unsalted pistachios are wonderful mixed with cooked rice or tossed into desserts (especially homemade ice creams).

For maximum flavor, lightly roast nuts first before chopping or crushing. Use them as crisp coatings too, but watch that they don't burn.

There is an increasing range of colorful and exciting seeds now in healthfood stores. Most useful are sunflower and sesame seeds, while pumpkin and melon seeds are most attractive scattered into salads or simply nibbled as a snack. Seeds for attractive garnish as well as flavor include poppy seeds, black mustard, fenugreek and caraway seeds. Most of all, nuts and seeds look simply stunning lined up in clean storage jars on kitchen

shelves, tempting you to toss them into a whole variety of appetizing dishes – both hot and cold.

Herbs

Wherever possible, try to use fresh herbs for cooking. There are many that will grow easily and obligingly in pots and small back gardens as well as surviving the winter cold. Good candidates include bush rosemary, thyme, bay and sage. Even chives and marjoram can survive well into late fall and then return to thrive again in early spring. However, more and more food shops are now selling packs and bunches of delicious fresh herbs which are grown commercially.

I find ethnic stores are great sources of good flavored and cheap herbs. Most useful are flat leaf parsley, coriander, dill, basil, chives and mint. Do not just use one herb per dish either. Mix, match and experiment and use in generous amounts; although the more pungent such as tarragon, rosemary and sage, still need a cautious touch.

Handfuls of fresh leafy herbs are wonderful tossed into green salads making them very exciting – no need to chop them finely either. Pack a mug with

washed sprigs then snip them roughly with scissors. Store leafy herbs loosely in plastic food bags in the fridge, spraying them lightly with water if they look limp. They spring back almost magically.

If you use dried herbs, then buy in small amounts and store in a dry, cool cupboard to retain their flavor. Replace dried herbs regularly as they soon lose their color and flavor and end up tasting rather like dried grass.

Spices

The vegetarian's best friend! Warm, aromatic, colorful and easy to use, spices can lift the simplest dish into the supreme bracket. It is a misconception to think spices are pungently hot. Most are not; it is really only those of the chilli family — including cayenne – that are. Some spices are useful for both sweet and savory dishes, such as nutmeg, cinnamon, mace, cloves, cardamom and ginger. Others, such as fenugreek, turmeric, paprika, cumin, coriander berries and chilli, are used for savory dishes.

Spices are made for experimenting. Gradually you will learn which are the most pungent and to your liking. Some have glorious colors, like turmeric and paprika, others have a distinctive flavor. Add in cautious pinches at first until you decide what you enjoy most.

Spices are best roasted or fried first to bring out the aromatic oils. This can be done either in a hot oven or a frying pan. Where possible, use the seeds or grains of spices first and grind them down in a small electric spice mill or a pestle and mortar. Saffron (a most expensive spice) is best soaked briefly in a little warm water or milk to bring out its true flavor and pretty color.

And don't restrict the use of spices to ethnic and exotic dishes. Add them to home cooked favorites – try macaroni and cheese with paprika and cumin or fried eggs sprinkled with mustard seeds.

SOUPS & STARTERS

Tantalizing appetizers range from traditional favorites – including soups that could be served either before a main course or on their own as a light and wholesome meal – to more exotic dishes for elegant dinners.

Vegetable Stock

Use this versatile stock as the basis for all good soups and sauces. If you have an extra large saucepan, or stock pot, why not make double the quantity and freeze several batches?

MAKES 10 CUPS
2 leeks, roughly chopped
3 stalks celery, roughly chopped
1 large onion, with skin, chopped
2 pieces fresh ginger root, chopped
3 garlic cloves, unpeeled
1 yellow pepper, seeded and chopped
1 parsnip, chopped
mushroom stems
tomato peelings
3 tbsp light soy sauce
3 bay leaves
bundle of parsley stalks
3 sprigs of fresh thyme
1 sprig of fresh rosemary
2 tsp salt
ground black pepper
15 cups cold water

1 Put all the ingredients into a very large saucepan or a stock pot.

2 Bring slowly to a boil, then lower the heat and simmer for 30 minutes, stirring from time to time.

3 Allow the liquid and vegetables to cool. Strain, discard the vegetables and the stock is ready to use. Alternatively, chill or freeze the stock and keep it to use as required.

CRISP CROÛTONS

Easy to make and simple to store, these croûtons add a delightful touch to fresh home made soups.

They are also an ideal way of using up stale bread. Speciality bread such as Ciabatta or baguettes can be thinly sliced to make the nicest, crunchiest croûtons, but everyday sliced loaves can be cut into interesting shapes for fun entertaining. Use a good quality, flavorless oil such as sunflower or groundnut, or for a fuller flavor brush with extra virgin olive oil. Alternatively, you could use a flavored oil such as one with garlic and herbs or chilli.

Preheat the oven to 400°F. Place the croûtons on a baking sheet, brush with your chosen oil than bake for about 15 minutes until golden and crisp. They crisp up further as they cool. Store them in an airtight container for up to a week. Reheat in a warm oven if liked, before serving.

Sweetcorn and Potato Chowder

This creamy, hearty and substantial soup is high in both fiber and flavor. It's wonderful served with thick crusty bread and topped with some melted Cheddar cheese.

SERVES 4
1 onion, chopped
1 garlic clove, crushed
1 medium size potato, chopped
2 stalks celery, sliced
1 small green pepper, seeded, halved and sliced
2 tbsp sunflower oil
2 tbsp butter
2½ cups stock or water
salt and ground black pepper
1¼ cups milk
1 × 7 oz can lima beans
1 × 11 oz can corn kernels
good pinch dried sage

1 Put the onion, garlic, potato, celery and green pepper into a large saucepan with the oil and butter.

2 Heat the ingredients until sizzling then turn the heat down to low. Cover and sweat the vegetables gently for 10 minutes, shaking the pan occasionally.

3 Pour in the stock or water, season to taste and bring to a boil. Turn down the heat, cover and simmer gently for about 15 minutes.

4 Add the milk, beans and corn – including their liquors – and the sage. Simmer again for 5 minutes. Check the seasoning and serve hot.

Triple Red Soup

Vibrant in color and taste, this soup is quickly made. Use a red onion – if you can find one – it will enhance the final appearance.

SERVES 4–6
1 red pepper, seeded and chopped
1 onion, chopped
1 garlic clove, crushed
2 tbsp olive oil
1 × 14 oz can chopped tomatoes
4 cups stock
2 tbsp long grain rice
2 tbsp Worcestershire sauce
1 × 7 oz can red kidney beans
1 tsp dried oregano
1 tsp sugar
salt and ground black pepper
fresh parsley, chopped, and Cheddar cheese, grated, to garnish

1 Put the pepper, onion, garlic and oil into a large saucepan. Heat until sizzling then turn down to low. Cover and cook gently for 5 minutes.

2 Add the rest of the ingredients, except the garnishes, and bring to a boil. Stir well, then simmer – covered – for 15 minutes. Check the seasoning, garnish and serve hot. Omit the Cheddar cheese for a vegan soup.

Chinese Tofu and Lettuce Soup

This light, clear soup is brimming with nourishing tasty pieces. Ideally, make this in a wok with home made vegetable stock.

SERVES 4
2 tbsp groundnut or sunflower oil
7 oz smoked or marinated tofu, cubed
3 scallions, sliced diagonally
2 garlic cloves, cut in thin strips
1 carrot, thinly sliced in rounds
5 cups stock
2 tbsp soy sauce
1 tbsp dry sherry or vermouth
1 tsp sugar
4 oz Oak leaf or Romaine lettuce, shredded
salt and ground black pepper

1 Heat the oil in a wok, then stir-fry the tofu cubes until browned. Drain and set aside on kitchen paper.

2 In the same oil, stir-fry the scallions, garlic and carrot for 2 minutes. Pour in the stock, soy sauce, sherry or vermouth and sugar.

3 Bring to a boil and cook for 1 minute or so. Stir in the lettuce until it just wilts. Add the tofu, season to taste and serve the soup immediately.

Spiced Indian Cauliflower Soup

Light and tasty, this creamy, mildly spicy soup is multi-purpose. It makes a wonderful warming first course, an appetizing quick meal and – when served chilled – is delicious for any summer menu.

SERVES 4–6
1 large potato, peeled and diced
1 small cauliflower, chopped
1 onion, chopped
1 tbsp sunflower oil
1 garlic clove, crushed
1 tbsp fresh ginger, grated
2 tsp ground turmeric
1 tsp cumin seeds
1 tsp black mustard seeds
2 tsp ground coriander
4 cups vegetable stock
1¼ cups natural yogurt
salt and ground black pepper
fresh coriander or parsley, to garnish

1 Put the potato, cauliflower and onion into a large saucepan with the oil and 3 tbsp water. Heat until hot and bubbling, then cover and turn the heat down. Continue cooking the mixture for about 10 minutes.

2 Add the garlic, ginger and spices. Stir well and cook for another 2 minutes, stirring occasionally. Pour in the stock and season well. Bring to a boil, then cover and simmer for about 20 minutes. Stir in the yogurt, season well and garnish with coriander or parsley.

Winter Warmer Soup

Simmer a selection of popular winter root vegetables together for a warming and satisfying soup. Its creamy taste comes from adding cream or yogurt just before serving.

SERVES 6
3 medium carrots, chopped
1 large potato, chopped
1 large parsnip, chopped
1 large turnip or small rutabaga, chopped
1 onion, chopped
2 tbsp sunflower oil
2 tbsp butter
6 cups water
salt and ground black pepper
1 piece fresh ginger root, peeled and
  grated
1¼ cups milk
3 tbsp heavy cream, sour cream or natural
  yogurt
2 tbsp fresh dill, chopped

1 Put the carrots, potato, parsnip, turnip or rutabaga and onion into a large saucepan with the oil and butter. Fry lightly, then cover and sweat the vegetables on a very low heat for 15 minutes, shaking the pan occasionally.

2 Pour in the water, bring to a boil and season well. Cover and simmer for 20 minutes until the vegetables are soft.

3 Strain the vegetables, reserving the stock, add the ginger and purée in a food processor or blender until smooth.

4 Return the purée and stock to the pan. Add the milk and stir while the soup gently reheats.

5 Remove from the heat, stir in the heavy cream, sour cream or yogurt plus the dill, lemon juice and extra seasoning, if necessary. Reheat the soup, if you wish, but do not allow it to boil as you do so, or it may curdle.

Egg Flower Soup

For the very best flavor, you do need to use a home made stock for this soup. The egg sets into pretty strands giving the soup a flowery look, hence the name.

SERVES 6
4 cups stock
3 tbsp light soy sauce
2 tbsp dry sherry or vermouth
3 scallions, diagonally sliced
small piece fresh ginger root, shredded
4 large lettuce leaves, shredded
1 tsp sesame seed oil
2 eggs, beaten
salt and ground black pepper
sesame seeds, to garnish

1 Pour the stock into a large saucepan. Add all the ingredients except the eggs and seeds. Bring to a boil and then cook for about 2 minutes.

2 Very carefully, pour the eggs in a thin, steady stream into the center of the boiling liquid.

3 Count to three then quickly stir the soup. The egg will begin to cook and form long threads. Season to taste, ladle the soup into warm bowls and serve immediately sprinkled with sesame seeds.

Broccoli and Saga Blue Cheese Soup

A popular vegetable, broccoli makes a delicious soup with an appetizing deep green color. For a tasty tang, stir in some cubes of Saga Blue cheese just before serving.

SERVES 6
1 onion, chopped
1 lb broccoli spears, chopped
1 large zucchini, chopped
1 large carrot, chopped
1 medium potato, chopped
2 tbsp butter
2 tbsp sunflower oil
8 cups stock or water
3 oz Saga Blue or Morbier cheese, cubed
salt and ground black pepper
almond flakes, to garnish (optional)

VARIATION

Try using cauliflower instead of broccoli in this recipe. Stilton also makes a tasty alternative to Saga Blue cheese.

1 Put all the vegetables into a large saucepan, together with the butter and oil plus about 3 tbsp stock or water.

2 Heat the ingredients until sizzling and stir well. Cover and cook gently for 15 minutes, shaking the pan occasionally, until all the vegetables soften.

3 Add the rest of the stock or water, season and bring to a boil, then cover and simmer gently for about 25–30 minutes.

4 Strain the vegetables and reserve the liquid. Purée the vegetables in a food processor or blender then return them to the pan with the reserved liquid.

5 Bring the soup back to a gentle boil and stir in the cheese until it melts. (Don't let the soup boil too hard or the cheese will become stringy.) Season to taste and garnish with a scattering of almond flakes.

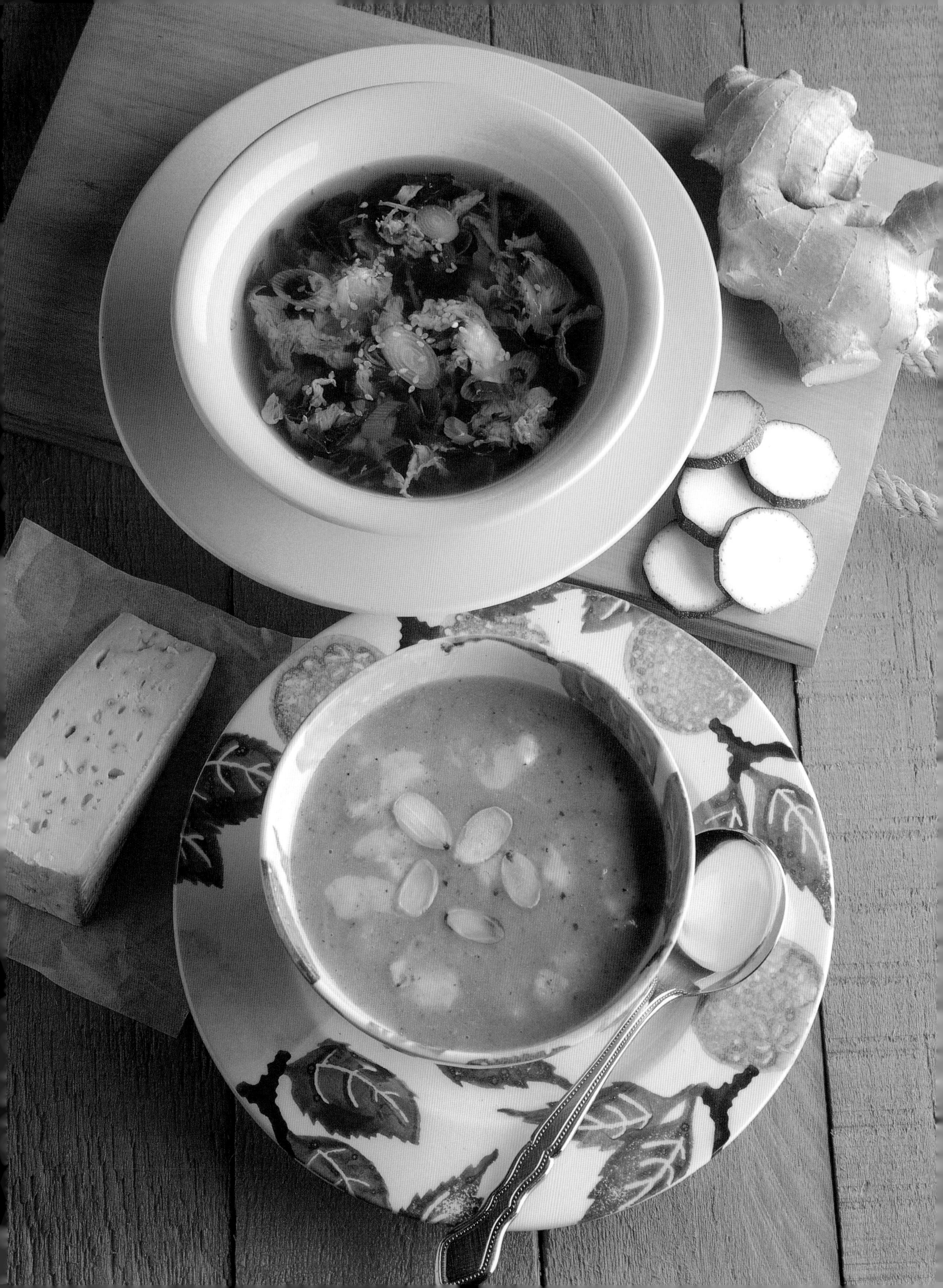

Cream of Mushroom Soup

Home made mushroom soup is quite different from canned or packaged soups. Add a few shiitake mushrooms (which are more readily available) to give your soup a richer flavor.

SERVES 4–6
1 lb white mushrooms, sliced
4 oz shiitake mushrooms, sliced
3 tbsp sunflower oil
1 onion, chopped
1 stalk celery, chopped
5 cups stock or water
2 tbsp soy sauce
¼ cup long grain rice
salt and ground black pepper
1¼ cups milk
fresh parsley, chopped, or almond flakes, to garnish

1 Put all the mushrooms into a large saucepan with the oil, onion and celery. Heat until sizzling, then cover and simmer for about 10 minutes, shaking the pan occasionally.

2 Add the stock or water, soy sauce, rice and seasoning. Bring to a boil then cover and simmer gently for 20 minutes until the vegetables and rice are soft.

3 Strain the vegetables, reserving the stock, and purée until smooth in a food processor or blender. Return the vegetables and reserved stock to the pan.

4 Stir in the milk, reheat until boiling and taste for seasoning. Serve hot sprinkled with a little chopped parsley and a few almond flakes.

Classic Minestrone

This famous Italian soup has been much imitated around the world – with varying results. The home made version is a delicious revelation and also extremely healthy with pasta, beans and fresh vegetables.

SERVES 4
1 large leek, thinly sliced
2 carrots, chopped
1 zucchini, thinly sliced
4 oz whole green beans, halved
2 stalks celery, thinly sliced
3 tbsp olive oil
6¼ cups stock or water
1 × 14 oz can chopped tomatoes
1 tbsp fresh basil, chopped
1 tsp fresh thyme leaves, chopped
  or ½ tsp dried thyme
salt and ground black pepper
1 × 14 oz can cannellini or kidney beans
⅓ cup small pasta shapes such as tubetti
  or macaroni
fresh Parmesan cheese, finely grated, to
  garnish (optional)
fresh parsley, chopped, to garnish

1 Put all the fresh vegetables into a large saucepan with the olive oil. Heat until sizzling then cover, lower the heat and sweat the vegetables for 15 minutes, shaking the pan occasionally.

2 Add the stock or water, tomatoes, herbs and seasoning. Bring to the boil, replace the lid and simmer gently for about 30 minutes.

3 Add the beans and their liquor together with the pasta, and simmer for a further 10 minutes. Check the seasoning and serve hot sprinkled with the Parmesan cheese (if used) and parsley.

COOK'S TIP

Minestrone is also delicious served cold on a hot summer's day. In fact the flavor improves if made a day or two ahead and stored in the refrigerator. It can also be frozen and reheated.

Borscht

A simply stunning color, this classic Russian soup is ideal to serve when you want to make something a little different. The flavor matures and improves too if it is made the day before it is needed.

SERVES 6
1 onion, chopped
1 lb raw beets, peeled and chopped
1 large cooking apple, chopped
2 celery stalks, chopped
½ red pepper, chopped
4 oz mushrooms, chopped
2 tbsp butter
2 tbsp sunflower oil
8 cups stock or water
1 tsp cumin seeds
pinch dried thyme
1 large bay leaf
fresh lemon juice
salt and ground black pepper
⅔ cup sour cream
few sprigs fresh dill, to garnish

1 Place all the chopped vegetables into a large saucepan with the butter, oil and 3 tbsp of the stock or water. Cover and cook gently for about 15 minutes, shaking the pan occasionally.

2 Stir in the cumin seeds and cook for a minute, then add the remaining stock or water, dried thyme, bay leaf, lemon juice and seasoning.

3 Bring to a boil, then cover and turn down to a gentle simmer. Cook for about 30 minutes.

4 Strain the vegetables and reserve the liquid. Pass the vegetables through a food processor or blender until they are smooth and creamy.

5 Return the vegetables to the pan, stir in the reserved stock and reheat. Check the seasoning.

6 Serve the borscht with swirls of sour cream and topped with a few sprigs of fresh dill.

VARIATION

This soup can be served fairly thick, as long as the vegetables are finely chopped first.

Beets are something of an under-valued vegetable, although popular in many European countries. For example, they are delicious served as a hot vegetable accompaniment with a bechamel sauce and topped with crisp bread crumbs. Alternatively, try them raw and coarsely grated, then tossed in dressing for a side salad.

Garlicky Mushrooms

Serve these on toast for a quick and tasty starter, or pop them into small ramekins and serve with slices of warm crusty bread. Use some shiitake mushrooms, if you can find them, for a richer flavor.

SERVES 4
1 lb button mushrooms, sliced if large
3 tbsp olive oil
3 tbsp stock or water
2 tbsp dry sherry (optional)
3 garlic cloves, crushed
4 oz low fat farmer's cheese
2 tbsp fresh parsley, chopped
1 tbsp fresh chives, chopped
salt and ground black pepper

1 Put the mushrooms into a large saucepan with the olive oil, stock or water and sherry, if using. Heat until bubbling then cover and simmer for 5 minutes.

2 Add the garlic and stir well. Cook for a further 2 minutes. Remove the mushrooms with a slotted spoon and set them aside. Cook the liquor until it reduces down to 2 tbsp. Remove from the heat and stir in the cheese and herbs.

3 Stir the mixture well until the cheese melts, then return the mushrooms to the pan so that they become coated with the cheese mixture. Season to taste.

4 Pile the mushrooms onto thick slices of hot toast. Alternatively, spoon them into four ramekins and serve accompanied by slices of crusty bread.

Ricotta and Borlotti Bean Pâté

A lovely light yet full-flavored pâté. For an attractive presentation, spoon the pâté into small, oiled ring molds, turn out and fill with some whole borlotti beans, simply dressed with lemon juice, olive oil and fresh herbs.

SERVES 4
1 × 14 oz can borlotti beans, drained
1 garlic clove, crushed
6 oz ricotta cheese (or other cream cheese)
4 tbsp butter, melted
juice of ½ lemon
salt and ground black pepper
2 tbsp fresh parsley, chopped
1 tbsp fresh thyme or dill, chopped
TO SERVE
extra canned beans (optional)
fresh lemon juice, olive oil and chopped herbs (optional)
salad leaves, radish slices and few sprigs fresh dill, to garnish

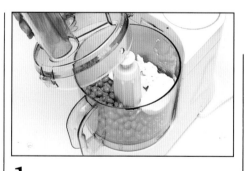

1 Blend the beans, garlic, cheese, butter, lemon juice and seasoning in a food processor until smooth.

2 Add the chopped herbs and continue to blend. Spoon into one serving dish or four lightly oiled ramekins, the bases lined with discs of waxed paper. Chill the pâté so that it sets firm.

3 If serving with extra beans, dress them with lemon juice, olive oil and herbs, season well and spoon on top. Garnish with salad leaves and serve with warm crusty bread or toast.

4 If serving individually, turn each pâté out of its ramekin onto a small plate and remove the disc of paper. Garnish with salad leaves, and top the pâtés with radish slices and sprigs of dill.

VARIATION

You could try other canned beans for this recipe, although the softer lentils would not be suitable. Lima beans are surprisingly good. For an attractive presentation fill the center with dark red kidney beans and chopped fresh green beans.

Mediterranean Vegetables with Tahini

Wonderfully colorful, this starter is easily prepared in advance. For an *al fresco* meal, why not grill the vegetables on a barbecue? Tahini is a paste made from sesame seeds.

SERVES 4
2 peppers, red, green or yellow, seeded and quartered
2 zucchini, halved lengthways
2 small eggplants, seeded and halved lengthwise
1 fennel bulb, quartered
olive oil
salt and ground black pepper
4 oz Greek Halloumi cheese, sliced
TAHINI CREAM
1 cup tahini paste
1 garlic cloves, crushed
2 tbsp olive oil
2 tbsp fresh lemon juice
½ cup cold water

1 Preheat the broiler or barbecue until hot. Brush the vegetables with the oil and broil until just browned, turning once. (If the peppers begin to blacken, don't worry. The skins can be peeled off.) Cook the vegetables until just softened.

2 Place the vegetables in a shallow dish and season. Allow to cool. Meanwhile, brush the cheese slices with oil and grill these on both sides until just charred. Remove them with a spatula.

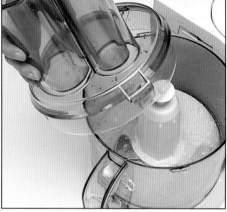

3 To make the tahini cream, place all the ingredients, except the water, in a food processor or blender. Whizz for a few seconds to mix, then, with the motor still running, pour in the water and blend until smooth.

4 Serve the vegetables and cheese on a platter and trickle over the cream. Delicious served with warm pitta or naan breads.

Imam Bayildi

Legend has it that a Muslim holy man – the Imam – was so overwhelmed by this dish that he fainted in sheer delight! Translated, Imam Bayildi means "The Imam fainted."

SERVES 4
2 medium eggplants, seeded (see Cook's Tip) and halved lengthwise
salt
4 tbsp olive oil
2 large onions, sliced thinly
2 garlic cloves, crushed
1 green pepper, seeded and sliced
1 × 14 oz can chopped tomatoes
1½ oz sugar
1 tsp ground coriander
ground black pepper
2 tbsp fresh coriander or parsley, chopped

1 Using a sharp knife, slash the flesh of the eggplants a few times. Sprinkle with salt and place in a colander for about half an hour. Rinse well and pat dry.

2 Gently fry the eggplants, cut side down, in the oil for 5 minutes, then drain and place in a shallow ovenproof dish.

3 In the same pan gently fry the onions, garlic and green pepper, adding extra oil if necessary. Cook for about 10 minutes, until the vegetables have softened.

4 Add the tomatoes, sugar, ground coriander and seasoning and cook for about 5 minutes until the mixture is reduced. Stir in the chopped coriander or parsley.

5 Spoon this mixture on top of the eggplants. Preheat the oven to 375°F, cover and bake for about 30–35 minutes. When cooked, cool, then chill. Serve cold with crusty bread.

COOK'S TIP

To prepare eggplants: sprinkle cut slices with salt and allow the juices that form to drain away in a colander. After 30 minutes or so, rinse well and pat dry. Eggplants prepared like this are less bitter and easier to cook.

Twice-baked Goat Cheese Soufflés

A good chef's trick is to reheat small baked soufflés out of their ramekins to serve with a salad. They puff up again and the outsides become nice and crispy. If you prefer, you can substitute another full-flavored cheese such as Cheddar or Parmesan.

SERVES 6
2 tbsp butter
3 tbsp all-purpose flour
1¼ cups hot milk
pinch cayenne pepper
squeeze of lemon juice
salt and ground black pepper
3½ oz semi-hard goat cheese, crumbled
2 eggs, separated
melted butter, for brushing
3 tbsp dried breadcrumbs
3 tbsp ground hazelnuts or walnuts
2 egg whites
salad garnish (optional)

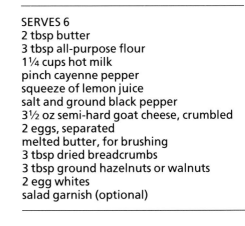

1 Melt the butter and stir in the flour. Cook to a roux for a minute then gradually whisk in the hot milk to make a thick white sauce.

VARIATION

There is another good chef's trick – making soufflés in advance and chilling them unbaked. It helps to add an extra egg white or two when whisking, depending on the mixture. It is also possible to freeze unbaked soufflés in small ramekins and then to bake them from frozen, allowing an extra 5 or 10 minutes' baking time.

2 Simmer for a minute then season with cayenne, lemon juice, salt and pepper. Remove the pan from the heat and stir in the cheese until it melts. Cool slightly then beat in the egg yolks.

3 Brush the insides of six ramekins with the melted butter and coat them with the breadcrumbs and nuts mixed together. Shake out any excess.

4 Preheat the oven to 375°F and prepare a bain marie – a roasting pan half-filled with boiling water.

5 Whisk the four egg whites to the soft peak stage and carefully fold them into the main mixture using a figure of eight motion. Spoon into the ramekins.

6 Place the soufflés in the bain marie and bake for about 12–15 minutes until risen and golden brown. You can of course serve them at this stage; otherwise allow to cool then chill.

7 To serve twice-baked, reheat the oven to the same temperature. Run a knife round the inside of each ramekin and turn out each soufflé onto a baking tray.

8 Bake the soufflés for about 12 minutes. Serve on prepared plates with a dressed salad garnish.

Tricolor Salad

This can be a simple starter if served on individual salad plates, or part of a light buffet meal laid out on a platter. When lightly salted, tomatoes make their own flavorsome dressing with their natural juices.

SERVES 4—6
1 small red onion, sliced thinly
6 large full-flavored tomatoes
extra virgin olive oil, to sprinkle
2 oz/small bunch rocket or watercress, roughly chopped
salt and ground black pepper
6 oz Mozzarella cheese, thinly sliced or grated
2 tbsp pine nuts (optional)

1 Soak the onion slices in a bowl of cold water for 30 minutes, then drain and pat dry. Skin the tomatoes by slashing and dipping briefly in boiling water. Remove the core and slice the flesh.

2 Slice the tomatoes and arrange half on a large platter, or divide them between small plates.

3 Sprinkle liberally with olive oil, then layer with the chopped rocket or cress and soaked onion slices, seasoning well. Add in the cheese, sprinkling over more oil and seasoning as you go.

4 Repeat with the remaining tomato slices, salad leaves, cheese and oil.

5 Season well to finish and complete with some oil and a good scattering of pine nuts. Cover the salad and chill for at least 2 hours before serving.

Guacamole Salsa in Red Leaves

This lovely, light summery starter looks so attractive arranged in cups of radicchio leaves. Serve with chunks of warm garlic bread.

SERVES 4
2 tomatoes, skinned and chopped
1 tbsp grated onion
1 garlic clove, crushed
1 green chili, halved, seeded and chopped
2 ripe avocadoes
2 tbsp olive oil
½ tsp ground cumin
2 tbsp fresh coriander or parsley, chopped
juice of 1 lime
salt and ground black pepper
leaves from radicchio lettuce

1 Using a sharp knife, slash a small cross on the top of the tomatoes, then dip them briefly in a bowl of boiling water. The skins will slip off easily. Remove the core and chop the flesh.

2 Put the tomato flesh into a bowl together with the onion, garlic and chopped chili. Halve and pit the avocadoes, then scoop the flesh into the bowl, mashing it with a fork.

3 Add the remaining ingredients, except for the radicchio leaves, and mix well together, seasoning to taste.

4 Lay the radicchio leaves on a platter and spoon in the salsa. Serve immediately as avocadoes go black when exposed to the air.

COOK'S TIP

Take care when cutting chilies. The juice can sting, so be careful not to rub your eyes until you have washed your hands.

Stuffed Artichokes

Artichokes are a little fussy to prepare but their delicious taste makes it all worthwhile, especially when they are stuffed with nuts, mushrooms and sun-dried tomatoes. This dish can be prepared in advance and reheated before serving.

SERVES 4
4 medium artichokes
salt
lemon slices
STUFFING
1 medium onion, chopped
1 garlic clove, crushed
3 tbsp olive oil
4 oz mushrooms, chopped
1 medium carrot, grated
1½ oz sun-dried tomatoes in oil, drained and sliced
leaves from a sprig of thyme
about 3–4 tbsp water
ground black pepper
2 cups fresh bread crumbs
extra olive oil, to cook
fresh parsley, chopped, to garnish

1 Boil the artichokes in plenty of salted water with a few slices of lemon for about 30 minutes, or until a leaf pulls easily from the base. Strain through a colander and cool the artichokes, setting them upside down.

2 To make the stuffing for the artichokes, gently fry the onion and garlic in the oil for 5 minutes, then add the mushrooms, carrot, sun-dried tomatoes and thyme.

3 Stir in the water, season well and cook for a further 5 minutes, then mix in the bread crumbs.

VARIATION

For a simpler meal, rather than stuff the artichokes, you could simply fill the centers with home made mayonnaise or serve with a dish of vinaigrette or melted butter for dipping the leaves.

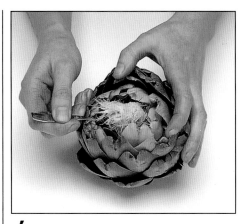

4 Taking each artichoke in turn, pull the leaves apart and pull out the purple-tipped central leaves. Using a small teaspoon, scrape out the hairy choke, making sure that you remove it all.

5 Spoon the stuffing into the center of each artichoke, and push the leaves back into shape. Put the artichokes into an ovenproof dish and pour a little oil into the center of each one.

6 One-half hour before serving, heat the oven to 375°F and bake the artichokes for about 20–25 minutes until heated through. Serve garnished with a little chopped fresh parsley on top.

Bruschetta with Goat Cheese and Tapenade

Simple to prepare in advance, this appetizing dish can be served as a starter or at finger buffets. Make sure that you finely chop the ingredients for the tapenade.

SERVES 4–6
TAPENADE
1 × 14 oz can black olives, pitted and finely chopped
2 oz sun-dried tomatoes in oil, chopped
2 tbsp capers, chopped
1 tbsp green peppercorns, in brine, crushed
3–4 tbsp olive oil
2 garlic cloves, crushed
3 tbsp fresh basil, chopped, or 1 tsp dried basil
salt and ground black pepper
BASES
12 slices Ciabatta or other crusty bread
olive oil, for brushing
2 garlic cloves, halved
4 oz soft goat cheese (or plain cream cheese)
fresh herb sprigs, to garnish

1 Mix the tapenade ingredients all together and check the seasoning. It should not need too much. Allow to marinate overnight, if possible.

2 To make the bruschetta, grill both sides of the bread lightly until golden. Brush one side with oil and then rub with a cut clove of garlic. Set aside until ready to serve.

3 Spread the bruschetta with the cheese, roughing it up with a fork, and spoon the tapenade on top. Garnish with sprigs of herbs.

COOK'S TIP

The bruschetta is tastiest broiled over an open barbecue flame, if possible. Failing that a broiler will do, but avoid using a toaster – it gives too even a color and the bruschetta is supposed to have a smoky flavor.

Warm Avocadoes with Tangy Topping

Lightly grilled with a tasty topping of red onions and cheese, this dish makes a delightful alternative to the rather humdrum avocado vinaigrette.

SERVES 4
1 small red onion, sliced
1 garlic clove, crushed
1 tbsp sunflower oil
Worcestershire sauce
2 ripe avocados, halved and pitted
2 small tomatoes, sliced
1 tbsp fresh chopped basil, marjoram or parsley
2 oz Lancashire or Mozzarella cheese, sliced
salt and ground black pepper

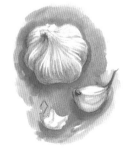

1 Gently fry the onion and garlic in the oil for about 5 minutes until just softened. Shake in a little Worcestershire sauce.

2 Preheat a broiler. Place the avocado halves on the broiling pan and spoon the onions into the center.

3 Divide the tomato slices and fresh herbs between the four halves and top each one with the cheese.

4 Season well and broil until the cheese melts and starts to brown.

VARIATION

Avocadoes are wonderful served in other hot dishes too. Try them chopped and tossed into hot pasta or sliced and layered in a lasagne.

Tempura Vegetables with Dipping Sauce

A Japanese favorite, these are thinly sliced, fresh vegetables fried in a light crispy batter and served with a small bowl of flavored soy sauce. For the best results, serve these immediately so the batter remains crisp. Tempura also makes a delicious party piece.

SERVES 4–6
1 medium zucchini, sliced in thin sticks
1 red pepper, seeded and cut in wedges
3 large mushrooms, quartered
1 fennel bulb, cut in wedges with root attached
½ medium eggplant, thinly sliced
oil, for deep frying
SAUCE
3 tbsp soy sauce
1 tbsp medium dry sherry
1 tsp sesame seed oil
few shreds fresh ginger or scallion
BATTER
1 egg
1 cup all-purpose flour
¾ cup cold water
salt and ground black pepper

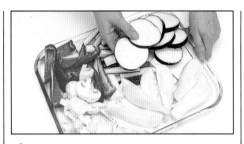

1 Prepare all the vegetables and lay them out on a tray, together with sheets of paper towel for draining the vegetables after cooking.

2 Mix the sauce ingredients together by whisking them in a bowl or shaking them together in a sealed jar. Pour into a bowl.

3 Half fill a deep frying pan with oil and preheat to a temperature of about 375°F. Quickly whisk the batter ingredients together but don't overbeat them. It doesn't matter if the batter is a little lumpy.

4 Fry the vegetables in stages by dipping a few quickly into the batter and lowering into the hot oil in a wire basket. Fry for just a minute until golden brown and crisp. Drain on the paper towel.

5 Repeat until all the vegetables are fried. Keep those you have cooked, uncovered, in a warm oven while you fry the rest. Serve the vegetables on a large platter alongside the dipping sauce.

COOK'S TIP

Successful deep frying can be quite tricky and a bit hazardous. First, be sure never to leave the pan of oil unattended while the heat is turned on. If you have to leave the stove, then turn the oil off. The oil will drop in temperature during cooking so keep re-heating it between batches.

Corn Blinis with Dill Cream

A mouth-watering and unusual starter, these blinis are also suitable for a cocktail buffet. Ideally make them an hour or two before you serve them, although the batter will stand for longer.

SERVES 6—8
¾ cup all-purpose flour
⅔ cup whole wheat flour
1 cup buttermilk
4 small eggs, beaten
½ tsp salt
½ tsp baking powder
2 tbsp butter, melted
good pinch baking soda
1 tbsp hot water
1 × 7 oz can corn kernels, drained
oil, for the griddle
DILL CREAM
7 oz sour cream
2 tbsp fresh dill, chopped
2 tbsp fresh chives, chopped
salt and ground black pepper

1 Mix the two flours and buttermilk together until completely smooth. Cover and leave to chill for about 8 hours in the refrigerator.

2 Beat in the eggs, salt, baking powder and butter. Mix the baking soda with the hot water and add this too, along with the corn kernels.

3 Heat a griddle or heavy based frying pan until quite hot. Brush with a little oil and drop spoonfuls of the blinis mixture on to it. The mixture should start to sizzle immediately.

4 Cook until holes appear on the top and the mixture looks almost set. Using a spatula, flip the blinis over and cook briefly. Stack the blinis under a clean dish towel while you make the rest.

5 To make the cream, simply blend the sour cream with the herbs and seasoning. Serve the blinis with a few spoonfuls of cream and garnished with sliced radishes and herbs.

LIGHT LUNCHES & SUPPERS

For tempting lunches that are not too filling and tasty television suppers, experiment with these glorious recipes, from those that include protein-rich ingredients such as tofu to irresistible cheese and pasta dishes.

Mexican Brunch Eggs

Instead of eggs on toast, why not try them on fried corn tortillas with chilies and creamy avocado? Packaged tortillas are readily available from larger supermarkets or delicatessens.

SERVES 4
oil, for frying
8 tortilla corn pancakes
1 avocado
1 large tomato
4 tbsp butter
8 eggs
4 jalepeno chilies, either fresh or
   canned, sliced
salt and ground black pepper
1 tbsp fresh coriander, chopped,
   to garnish

1 Heat the oil and fry the tortillas for a few seconds each side. Remove and drain. Keep the tortillas warm.

2 Halve, pit and peel the avocado, then cut into slices. Dip the tomato into boiling water, then skin and chop roughly.

3 Melt the butter in a frying pan and fry the eggs, in batches, sunny side up.

4 Place two tortillas on four plates, slip an egg on each and top with sliced chilies, avocado and tomato. Season and serve garnished with fresh coriander.

Fried Tomatoes with Polenta Crust

If you saw the film "Fried Green Tomatoes" then you should enjoy this dish! No need to search for home-grown green tomatoes – any slightly under-ripe ones will do.

SERVES 4
4 large firm under-ripe tomatoes
1 cup polenta or coarse cornmeal
1 tsp dried oregano
½ tsp garlic powder
all-purpose flour, for dredging
1 egg, beaten with seasoning
oil, for deep fat frying

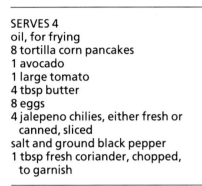

1 Cut the tomatoes into thick slices. Mix the polenta or cornmeal with the oregano and garlic powder.

2 Put the flour, egg and polenta or cornmeal into bowls. Dip the tomato slices into the flour, then into the egg and finally into the polenta or cornmeal.

3 Fill a shallow frying pan one-third full of oil and heat steadily until quite hot.

4 Slip the tomato slices into the oil carefully, a few at a time, and fry on each side until crisp. Remove and drain. Repeat with the remaining tomatoes, reheating the oil in between. Serve with salad.

Mushroom and Chili Carbonara

For a richer mushroom flavor, use a small package of dried Italian porcini mushrooms in this quick egg sauce, and for an extra spicy zing, toss in some chili flakes too.

SERVES 4
1 × ½ oz package dried porcini mushrooms
1¼ cups hot water
8 oz spaghetti
1 garlic clove, crushed
2 tbsp butter
1 tbsp olive oil
8 oz button or field mushrooms, sliced
1 tsp dried chili flakes
2 eggs
1¼ cups light cream
salt and ground black pepper
fresh Parmesan cheese, grated, and parsley, chopped, to serve

1 Soak the dried mushrooms in the hot water for 15 minutes, drain and reserve the liquor.

2 Boil the spaghetti according to the instructions on the package in salted water. Drain and rinse in cold water.

3 In a large saucepan, lightly sauté the garlic with the butter and oil for half a minute then add the mushrooms, including the soaked porcini ones, and the dried chili flakes, and stir well. Cook for about 2 minutes, stirring a few times.

4 Pour in the reserved mushroom stock and boil to reduce slightly.

5 Beat the eggs with the cream and season well. Return the cooked spaghetti to the pan and toss in the eggs and cream. Reheat, without boiling, and serve hot sprinkled with Parmesan cheese and chopped parsley.

VARIATION

Instead of mushrooms, try using either finely sliced and sautéed leeks or perhaps coarsely shredded lettuce with peas. If chili flakes are too hot and spicy for you, then try the delicious alternative of skinned and chopped tomatoes with torn, fresh basil leaves.

Tagliatelle with Hit-the-pan Salsa

It is possible to make a hot filling meal within just fifteen minutes with this quick-cook salsa sauce. If you don't have time to peel the tomatoes, then don't bother.

SERVES 2
8 oz tagliatelle
3 tbsp olive oil, preferably extra virgin
3 large tomatoes
1 garlic clove, crushed
4 scallions, sliced
1 green chili, halved, seeded and sliced
juice of 1 orange (optional)
2 tbsp fresh parsley, chopped
salt and ground black pepper
cheese, grated, to garnish (optional)

1 Boil the tagliatelle in plenty of salted water until it is *al dente*. Drain and toss in a little of the oil. Season well.

2 Skin the tomatoes by dipping them briefly in a bowl of boiling water. The skins should slip off easily. Chop the tomatoes roughly.

3 Heat the remaining oil until it is quite hot and stir-fry the garlic, onions and chili for a minute. The pan should sizzle.

4 Add the tomatoes, orange juice (if using) and parsley. Season well and stir in the tagliatelle to reheat. Serve with the grated cheese (if used).

COOK'S TIP

You could use any pasta shape for this recipe. It would be particularly good with large rigatoni or linguini, or as a sauce for fresh ravioli or tortellini.

Potato and Cabbage Croquettes

This London breakfast dish is enjoying something of a revival. Originally made on Mondays with leftover potatoes and cabbage from the Sunday lunch, it is suitable for any light meal occasion. For breakfast, serve the croquettes with eggs, grilled tomatoes and mushrooms.

SERVES 4
1 lb/3 cups mashed potato
8 oz steamed or boiled cabbage or kale, shredded
1 egg, beaten
4 oz Cheddar cheese, grated
fresh nutmeg, grated
salt and ground black pepper
all-purpose flour, for coating
oil, for frying

1 Mix the potatoes with the cabbage or kale, egg, cheese, nutmeg and seasoning. Divide and shape into eight croquettes.

2 Chill for an hour or so, if possible, as this enables the mixture to become firm and makes it easier to fry. Toss the croquettes in the flour. Heat about ½ in of oil in a frying pan until it is quite hot.

3 Carefully slide the croquettes into the oil and fry on each side for about 3 minutes until golden and crisp. Drain on paper towel and serve hot and crisp.

Cheese and Chutney Toasts

Quick cheese on toast can be made quite memorable with a few tasty additions. Serve these scrumptious toasties with a simple salad.

SERVES 4
4 slices whole wheat bread, thickly sliced
butter or margarine
4 oz Cheddar cheese, grated
1 tsp dried thyme
ground black pepper
2 tbsp chutney or relish

1 Preheat the broiler. Toast the bread slices lightly on each side, then spread sparingly with butter or margarine.

2 Mix the cheese and thyme together and season with pepper.

3 Spread the chutney or relish on the toast and divide the cheese between the four slices.

4 Return to the broiler and cook until browned and bubbling. Cut into halves, diagonally, and serve with salad.

Risotto Primavera

Real Italian risottos should be creamy and full of flavor. They are best made freshly and do need frequent stirring, but this can be done in between other jobs in the kitchen. For best results use a quality Arborio rice which has a good *al dente* bite.

SERVES 4
4 cups hot vegetable stock, preferably home made
1 red onion, chopped
2 garlic cloves, crushed
2 tbsp olive oil
2 tbsp butter
1¼ cups risotto rice (do not rinse)
3 tbsp dry white wine
4 oz asparagus spears or green beans, sliced and blanched
2 young carrots, sliced and blanched
2 oz baby button mushrooms
salt and ground black pepper
2 oz Pecorino or Parmesan cheese, grated

1 It is important to follow the steps for making real risotto so that you achieve the right texture. First, heat the stock in a saucepan to simmering.

2 Next to it, in a large saucepan, sauté the onion and garlic in the oil and butter for 3 minutes.

3 Stir in the rice, making sure each grain is coated well in the oil, then stir in the wine. Allow to reduce down and spoon in two ladles of hot stock, stirring continuously.

4 Allow this to bubble down, then add more stock and stir again. Continue like this, ladling in the stock and stirring frequently for up to 20 minutes, by which time the rice will have swelled greatly.

5 Mix in the asparagus or beans, carrots and mushrooms, seasoning well, and cook for a minute or two more. Serve immediately in bowls with a scattering of grated cheese.

VARIATION

If you have any leftover risotto, shape it into small balls and then coat in beaten egg and dried bread crumbs. Chill for 30 minutes before deep frying in hot oil until golden and crisp.

Kitchiri

This is the Indian original which inspired the classic breakfast dish known as kedgeree. Made with basmati rice and small tasty lentils this will make an ample supper or brunch dish.

SERVES 4
1 cup Indian masoor dhal or
  green lentils
1 garlic clove, crushed
4 tbsp vegetarian ghee or butter
2 tbsp sunflower oil
1¼ cups easy-cook basmati rice
2 tsp ground coriander
2 tsp cumin seeds
2 cloves
3 cardamom pods
2 bay leaves
1 stick cinnamon
4 cups stock
2 tbsp tomato paste
salt and ground black pepper
3 tbsp fresh coriander or parsley, chopped

1 Cover the dhal or lentils with boiling water and soak for 30 minutes. Drain and boil in fresh water for 10 minutes. Drain once more and set aside.

2 Fry the onion and garlic in the ghee or butter and oil in a large saucepan for about 5 minutes.

3 Add the rice, stir well to coat the grains in the ghee or butter and oil, then stir in the spices. Cook gently for a minute or so.

4 Add the lentils, stock, tomato paste and seasoning. Bring to a boil, then cover and simmer for 20 minutes until the stock is absorbed and the lentils and rice are just soft. Stir in the coriander or parsley and check the seasoning. Remove the cinnamon stick and bay leaf.

Pissaladière

A French Mediterranean classic, this is a delicious and colorful tart full of punchy flavor. Ideally, put the base and fillings together just when serving so the base remains crisp.

SERVES 6
PASTRY
2 cups all-purpose flour
½ cup butter or sunflower margarine, chilled
1 tsp dried mixed herbs
pinch salt
FILLING
2 large onions, thinly sliced
2 garlic cloves, crushed
3 tbsp olive oil
fresh nutmeg, grated, to taste
1 × 14 oz can chopped tomatoes
1 tsp sugar
leaves from small sprig of thyme
salt and ground black pepper
⅔ cup pitted black olives, sliced
2 tbsp capers
fresh parsley, chopped, to garnish

1 Rub the flour with the butter or margarine until it forms fine crumbs, then mix in the herbs and salt. Mix to a firm dough with cold water. Preheat the oven to 375°F.

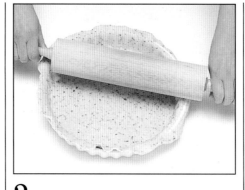

2 Roll out the crust and line a 9 in pie pan. Line with foil and dried beans and bake for 10 minutes. Remove foil and beans and bake for 5 minutes more.

3 Gently fry the onions and garlic in the oil for about 10 minutes until quite soft and mix in the nutmeg.

4 Stir in the tomatoes, sugar, thyme and seasoning and simmer gently for about 10 minutes until the mixture is reduced and slightly syrupy.

5 Remove from the heat and allow to cool. Mix in the olives and capers.

6 When ready to serve, spoon into the pie shell, sprinkle with some fresh chopped parsley and serve at room temperature.

VARIATION

To serve Pissaladière hot, top with grated cheese and broil until the cheese is golden and bubbling. The crisp-baked pastry shell can be used as a base for a number of other vegetable mixtures. Try filling it with a Russian Salad – chopped, cooked root vegetables, including potato and carrot, mixed with peas, beans and onions, blended with mayonnaise and sour cream. Top with slices of hard-boiled egg and garnish with chopped fresh herbs.

Multi Mushroom Stroganoff

A pan fry of sliced mushrooms swirled with sour cream is made especially interesting if two or three varieties of mushroom are used. It is even more delicious if you can incorporate woodland or wild mushrooms.

SERVES 3–4
3 tbsp olive oil
1 lb wild mushrooms (including ceps, shiitakes or oysters), sliced
3 scallions, sliced
2 garlic cloves, crushed
2 tbsp dry sherry or vermouth
salt and ground black pepper
1¼ cups sour cream or heavy cream
1 tbsp fresh marjoram or thyme leaves, chopped
fresh parsley, chopped

1 Heat the oil in a large frying pan and fry the mushrooms gently, stirring them occasionally until they are softened and just cooked.

2 Add the scallions, garlic and sherry or vermouth and cook for a minute more. Season well.

3 Stir in the sour cream or heavy cream and heat to just below boiling. Stir in the marjoram or thyme then scatter over the parsley. Serve with rice, pasta or boiled new potatoes.

Lima Bean and Pesto Pasta

Buy good quality, ready-made pesto, rather than making your own. Pesto forms the basis of several very tasty sauces, and it is especially good with lima beans.

SERVES 4
8 oz pasta shapes
salt and ground black pepper
fresh nutmeg, grated
2 tbsp extra virgin olive oil
1 × 14 oz can lima beans, drained
3 tbsp pesto sauce
⅔ cup light cream
TO SERVE
3 tbsp pine nuts
Parmesan cheese, grated (optional)
sprigs of fresh basil, to garnish (optional)

1 Boil the pasta until *al dente*, then drain, leaving it a little wet. Return the pasta to the pan, season, and stir in the nutmeg and oil.

2 Heat the beans in a saucepan with the pesto and cream, stirring until the cream begins to simmer. Toss the beans and pesto into the pasta and mix well.

3 Serve in bowls topped with pine nuts, and add a little grated cheese and basil sprigs if you wish.

Baked Potatoes and Three Fillings

Potatoes baked in their skins and packed with a variety of fillings make an excellent and nourishing meal. Although they have been cooked here in a conventional oven, potatoes can be baked more quickly and just as successfully in a microwave.

4 medium size baking potatoes
olive oil, for greasing
sea salt, to serve

1 Preheat the oven to 400°F. Score the potatoes with a cross and rub all over with the olive oil.

2 Place on a baking sheet and cook for 45–60 minutes until a knife inserted into the centers indicates they are cooked.

3 Cut the potatoes open along the score lines and push up the flesh from the base with your fingers. Season with salt and fill with your chosen filling.

EACH FILLING IS FOR FOUR POTATOES

RED BEAN FILLING
1 × 15 oz can red kidney beans
7 oz low fat cottage or cream cheese
2 tbsp mild chili sauce
1 tsp ground cumin

Red Bean – drain the beans, heat in a pan or microwave and stir in the cream cheese, chili sauce and cumin.

SOY VEGETABLES FILLING
2 leeks, thinly sliced
2 carrots, cut in sticks
1 zucchini, thinly sliced
4 oz baby corn, halved
3 tbsp groundnut or sunflower oil
4 oz button mushrooms, sliced
3 tbsp soy sauce
2 tbsp dry sherry or vermouth
1 tbsp sesame oil
sesame seeds, to sprinkle

Soy Vegetables – stir-fry the leeks, carrots, zucchini and baby corn in the oil for about 2 minutes, then add the mushrooms and cook for a further minute. Mix together the soy sauce, sherry and sesame oil and pour over the vegetables. Heat through until just bubbling and then scatter over the sesame seeds.

CHEESE AND CREAMED CORN FILLING
1 × 15 oz can creamed corn
4 oz cheese, grated
1 tsp dried mixed herbs

Cheese and creamed corn – heat the corn, add the cheese and mixed herbs.

Peanut Butter Fingers

Children will love these crispy, tasty croquettes. Make up a batch and freeze some ready for whenever there are young tummies to fill!

MAKES 12
2 lb potatoes
1 large onion, chopped
2 large peppers, red or green, chopped
3 carrots, coarsely grated
3 tbsp sunflower oil
2 zucchini, coarsely grated
4 oz mushrooms, chopped
1 tbsp dried mixed herbs
4 oz sharp Cheddar cheese, grated
½ cup crunchy peanut butter
salt and ground black pepper
2 eggs, beaten
about ½ cup dried breadcrumbs
3 tbsp grated Parmesan cheese
oil, for deep frying

1 Boil the potatoes until tender, then drain well and mash. Set aside.

2 Fry the onion, peppers and carrots gently in the oil for about 5 minutes then add the zucchini and mushrooms. Cook for 5 minutes more.

3 Mix the potato with the dried mixed herbs, grated cheese and peanut butter. Season, allow to cool for 30 minutes, then stir in one of the eggs.

4 Spread out on a large plate, cool and chill, then divide into 12 portions and shape. Dip your hands in cold water if the mixture sticks.

5 Put the second egg in a bowl and dip the potato fingers into it first, then into the crumbs and Parmesan cheese until coated evenly. Return to the fridge to set.

6 Heat the oil in a deep fat frier to 375°F then fry the fingers in batches for about 3 minutes until golden. Drain well on paper towel. Serve hot.

COOK'S TIP

To reheat, thaw for 1 hour, then oven bake at 375°F for 15 minutes.

Pasta Salade Tiède

Boil a pan of pasta shapes and toss with vinaigrette dressing and some freshly prepared salad vegetables, and you have the basis for a delicious warm salad.

SERVES 2
4 oz pasta shapes, e.g. shells
3 tbsp vinaigrette dressing
3 sun-dried tomatoes in oil, snipped
2 scallions, sliced
2 or 3 sprigs watercress or arugula, chopped
¼ cucumber, halved, seeded and sliced
salt and ground black pepper
about 1½ oz Pecorino cheese, coarsely grated

1 Boil the pasta according to the instructions on the package. Drain and toss in the dressing.

2 Mix in the tomatoes, onions, cress or arugula and cucumber. Season to taste.

3 Divide between two plates and sprinkle over the cheese. Eat at room temperature, if possible.

Penne with "Can Can" Sauce

The quality of canned beans and tomatoes is so good that it is possible to transform them into a very fresh tasting pasta sauce in minutes. Again, choose whatever pasta you like.

SERVES 3—4
8 oz penne pasta
1 onion, sliced
1 red pepper, seeded and sliced
2 tbsp olive oil
1 × 14 oz can chopped tomatoes
1 × 15 oz can chick peas
2 tbsp dry vermouth (optional)
1 tsp dried oregano
1 large bay leaf
2 tbsp capers
salt and ground black pepper

1 Boil the pasta as instructed on the package, then drain. In a saucepan, gently fry the onion and pepper in the oil for about 5 minutes, stirring occasionally, until softened.

2 Add the tomatoes, chick peas with their liquor, vermouth (if liked), herbs and capers.

3 Season and bring to a boil then simmer for about 10 minutes. Remove the bay leaf and mix in the pasta, reheat and serve hot.

Tofu and Crunchy Vegetables

High protein, wonder food tofu is nicest if marinated lightly before cooking. If you use the smoked tofu, it's even tastier. For successful stir-frying, make sure all your ingredients are prepared first.

SERVES 4
2 × 8 oz cartons smoked tofu, cubed
3 tbsp soy sauce
2 tbsp dry sherry or vermouth
1 tbsp sesame oil
3 tbsp groundnut or sunflower oil
2 leeks, thinly sliced
2 carrots, cut in sticks
1 large zucchini, thinly sliced
4 oz baby corn, halved
4 oz button or shiitake mushrooms, sliced
1 tbsp sesame seeds
1 package of egg noodles, cooked

1 Marinate the tofu in the soy sauce, sherry or vermouth and sesame oil for at least half an hour. Drain and reserve the marinade.

2 Heat the groundnut or sunflower oil in a wok and stir-fry the tofu cubes until browned all over. Remove and reserve.

3 Stir-fry the leeks, carrots, zucchini and baby corn, stirring and tossing for about 2 minutes. Add the mushrooms and cook for a further minute.

4 Return the tofu to the wok and pour in the marinade. Heat until bubbling, then scatter over the sesame seeds.

5 Serve as soon as possible with the hot cooked noodles, dressed in a little sesame oil, if liked.

VARIATION

Tofu is also excellent marinated and skewered, then lightly grilled. Push the tofu off the skewers into pockets of pitta bread. Fill with lemon-dressed salad and serve with a final trickle of tahini cream.

Egg Foo Yung

A great way of turning a bowl of leftover cooked rice into a meal for four, this Oriental dish is tasty and full of texture. Use bought bean sprouts or grow your own – it's easy and fun.

SERVES 4
salt and ground black pepper
3 eggs, beaten
good pinch five spice powder (optional)
3 tbsp groundnut or sunflower oil
4 scallions, sliced
1 garlic clove, crushed
1 small green pepper, seeded and chopped
4 oz fresh bean sprouts
3 cups cooked white rice
3 tbsp light soy sauce
1 tbsp sesame oil

1 Season the eggs and beat in the five spice powder, if using.

2 In a wok or large frying pan, heat one tablespoon of the oil and when quite hot, pour in the egg.

3 Cook rather like an omelet, pulling the mixture away from the sides and allowing the rest to slip underneath.

4 Cook the egg until firm then tip out. Chop the "omelet" into small strips.

5 Heat the remaining oil and stir-fry the scallions, garlic, pepper and bean sprouts for about 2 minutes, stirring and tossing continuously.

6 Mix in the rice and heat thoroughly, stirring well. Add the soy sauce and sesame oil then return the egg and mix in well. Serve immediately, piping hot.

Eggs Benedict with Quick Hollandaise

Traditional Hollandaise sauce is tricky to make without it curdling. To make it quickly, yet still achieve a thick and creamy sauce, use a blender or food processor. Hollandaise sauce is simply delicious served over poached eggs on hot toasted muffins.

SERVES 4
2 egg yolks
1 tsp dry mustard
good pinch each salt and ground black pepper
1 tbsp wine vinegar or lemon juice
¾ cup butter
4 muffins, split
butter or low fat spread
4 large eggs
2 tbsp capers
a little fresh parsley, chopped, to garnish

1 Blend the egg yolks with the mustard and seasoning in a blender or food processor for a few seconds until well mixed. Mix in the vinegar or lemon juice.

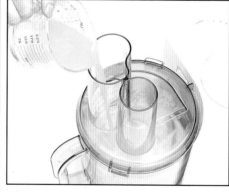

2 Heat the butter until it is on the point of bubbling then, with the machine still running, slowly pour the butter onto the egg yolks.

3 The mixture should emulsify instantly and become thick and creamy. Switch off the blender and set the sauce aside.

4 Toast the split muffins. Cut four of the halves in two and lightly butter. Place the four uncut halves on warmed plates and leave unbuttered.

5 Poach the eggs either in gently simmering water or in an egg poacher. Drain well and slip carefully onto the uncut muffin halves.

6 Spoon the sauce over the muffins and then sprinkle with capers and parsley. Serve immediately with the buttered muffin quarters.

VARIATION

This classic American brunch dish is said to have originated in New York, and is ideal to serve on a special occasion such as a birthday treat or New Year's day.

Instead of the toasted muffin, you could make more of a main meal by serving the dish on a bed of lightly steamed or blanched spinach mixed with quick fried sliced mushrooms and onions. The quick Hollandaise sauce is of course ideal as an all-purpose serving sauce for vegetables, baked potatoes, cauliflower and broccoli.

Light Ratatouille

This lightly cooked medley of fresh vegetables is cooked with simple poached eggs and served topped with crisply fried bread crumbs.

SERVES 4
3 tbsp olive oil
1 cup fresh white bread crumbs
1 yellow or red pepper, seeded and thinly sliced
2 garlic cloves, crushed
2 leeks, thinly sliced
2 zucchini, thinly sliced
2 tomatoes, skinned and sliced
1 tsp dried rosemary, crushed
4 eggs
salt and ground black pepper

1 Heat half the oil in a shallow fireproof dish (or frying pan with a lid) and fry the bread crumbs until they are golden and crisp. Drain on paper towel.

2 Add the remaining oil and fry the pepper, garlic and leeks in the same pan for about 10 minutes until softened.

3 Add the zucchini, tomatoes and rosemary and cook for a further 5 minutes. Season well.

4 Using the back of a spoon, make four wells in the vegetable mixture and break an egg into each one. Lightly season the eggs then cover and cook on a gentle heat for about 3 minutes until they are just set.

5 Sprinkle over the crisp bread crumbs and serve immediately, piping hot.

Macaroni Soufflé

This is generally a great favorite with children, and is rather like a light and fluffy macaroni and cheese. Make sure you serve a soufflé the moment it is cooked or it will sink dramatically.

SERVES 3–4
6 oz short cut macaroni
melted butter, to coat
6 tbsp dried bread crumbs
8 tbsp butter
2 tsp ground paprika
⅔ cup all-purpose flour
2½ cups milk
6 oz Cheddar or Gruyère cheese, grated
4 oz Parmesan cheese, grated
salt and ground black pepper
6 eggs, separated

1 Preheat the oven to 300°F. Boil the macaroni according to the package instructions. Drain and set aside.

2 Brush the insides of a 1 quart soufflé dish with melted butter and then coat evenly with the bread crumbs, shaking out any excess.

3 Put the butter, paprika, flour and milk into a saucepan and bring to a boil slowly, whisking it constantly until it is smooth and thick.

4 Simmer the sauce for a minute, then take off the heat and stir in the cheeses until they melt. Season well and mix with the macaroni.

5 Beat in the egg yolks. Whisk the egg whites until they form soft peaks and spoon a quarter into the sauce mixture, beating it gently to loosen it up.

6 Using a large metal spoon, carefully fold in the rest of the egg whites and transfer to the prepared soufflé dish.

7 Bake in the center of the oven for about 40–45 minutes until the soufflé has risen and is golden brown. The middle should wobble very slightly and the soufflé should be lightly creamy inside.

Cowboy Hot Pot

A great dish to serve as a children's main meal, which adults will enjoy too – if they are allowed to join the posse. You can use any vegetable mixture you like, although beans are a must for every self-respecting cowboy!

SERVES 4–6
1 onion, sliced
1 red pepper, sliced
1 sweet potato or 2 carrots, chopped
3 tbsp sunflower oil
4 oz green beans, chopped
1 × 14 oz can baked beans
1 × 7 oz can corn
1 tbsp tomato paste
1 tsp barbecue spice seasoning
4 oz Gouda or Edam cheese (preferably smoked), cubed
1 lb potatoes, thinly sliced
2 tbsp butter, melted
salt and ground black pepper

1 Fry the onion, pepper and sweet potato or carrots gently in the oil until softened but not browned.

2 Add the green beans, baked beans, corn (and liquor), tomato paste and barbecue spice seasoning. Bring to a boil, then simmer for 5 minutes.

3 Transfer the vegetables to a shallow ovenproof dish and then scatter with the cubed cheese.

4 Cover the vegetable and cheese mixture with the sliced potato, brush with butter, season and then bake at 375°F for 30–40 minutes until golden brown on top and the potato is cooked.

Stir-fried Rice and Vegetables

If you have some left-over cooked rice and a few vegetables lurking at the bottom of the refrigerator, then you've got the basis for this quick and tasty meal.

SERVES 4
½ cucumber
2 scallions, sliced
1 garlic clove, crushed
2 carrots, thinly sliced
1 small red or yellow pepper, seeded and sliced
3 tbsp sunflower or groundnut oil
¼ small green cabbage, shredded
4 cups cooked long grain rice
2 tbsp light soy sauce
1 tbsp sesame oil
salt and ground black pepper
fresh parsley or coriander, chopped (optional)
4 oz unsalted cashew nuts, almonds or peanuts

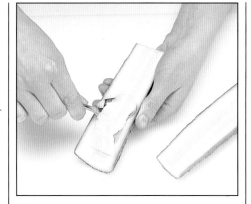

1 Halve the cucumber lengthwise and scoop out the seeds with a teaspoon. Slice the flesh diagonally. Set aside.

2 In a wok or large frying pan, stir-fry the scallions, garlic, carrots and pepper in the oil for about 3 minutes until they are just soft.

3 Add the cabbage and cucumber and fry for another minute or two until the leaves begin to just wilt. Mix in the rice, soy sauce, sesame oil and seasoning. Reheat the mixture thoroughly, stirring and tossing all the time.

4 Add the herbs, if using, and nuts. Check the seasoning and serve piping hot.

Pepper and Potato Tortilla

A great favorite with my family, tortilla is rather like a thick omelette or pastry-less quiche. Traditionally a Spanish dish, it is best eaten cold in chunky wedges. Tortilla makes ideal picnicking food. Use a hard Spanish cheese, like Mahon, or a goat cheese, if you can, although sharp Cheddar makes a good substitute.

SERVES 4
2 medium size potatoes
3 tbsp olive oil
1 large onion, thinly sliced
2 garlic cloves, crushed
2 peppers, one green and one red, thinly sliced
6 eggs, beaten
4 oz sharp cheese, grated
salt and ground black pepper

1 Do not peel the potatoes, but wash them thoroughly. Par boil them as they are for about 10 minutes, then drain and slice them thickly. Switch on the broiler so that it has time to warm up while you prepare the tortilla.

2 In a large non-stick or well seasoned frying pan, heat the oil and fry the onion, garlic and peppers on a moderate heat for 5 minutes until softened.

3 Add the potatoes and continue frying, stirring occasionally until the potatoes are completely cooked and the vegetables are soft. Add a little extra oil if the pan seems rather dry.

4 Pour in half the eggs, then sprinkle over half the cheese then the rest of the egg, seasoning as you go. Finish with a layer of cheese.

5 Continue to cook on a low heat, without stirring, half covering the pan with a lid to help set the eggs.

6 When the mixture is firm, flash the pan under the hot broiler to seal the top just lightly. Leave the tortilla in the pan to cool. This helps it firm up further and makes it easier to turn out.

VARIATION

You can add any sliced and lightly cooked vegetable, such as mushrooms, zucchini or broccoli, to this tortilla dish instead of the green and red peppers. Cooked pasta or brown rice are both excellent alternatives too.

Cauliflower and Egg Casserole

No need to make a traditional bechamel sauce for this country classic. A quick all-in-one sauce can be made in minutes while a small package of soup croûtons gives the dish a delicious crunchy topping.

SERVES 4
1 medium size cauliflower, broken in
   florets
1 medium onion, sliced
2 eggs, hard boiled, peeled and chopped
3 tbsp whole wheat flour
1 tsp mild curry powder
2 tbsp sunflower margarine or other low
   fat spread
2 cups milk
½ tsp dried thyme
salt and ground black pepper
4 oz sharp cheese, grated
small package of soup croûtons

1 Boil the cauliflower and onion in enough salted water to cover until they are just tender. Be careful not to overcook them. Drain well.

2 Arrange the cauliflower and onion in a shallow ovenproof dish and scatter over the chopped egg.

3 Put the flour, curry powder, fat and milk in a saucepan all together. Bring slowly to a boil, stirring well until thickened and smooth. Stir in the thyme and seasoning and allow the sauce to simmer for a minute or two. Remove the pan from the heat and stir in about three quarters of the cheese.

4 Pour the sauce over the cauliflower, scatter over the croûtons and sprinkle with the remaining cheese. Brown under a hot broiler until golden and serve. Delicious with thick crusty bread.

Quick Basmati and Nut Pilaf

Light and fragrant basmati rice from the foothills of the Himalayas cooks perfectly using this simple pilaf method. Use whatever nuts are your favorite – even unsalted peanuts are good, although almonds, cashews or pistachios are more exotic.

SERVES 4–6
1¼ cups basmati rice
1 onion, chopped
1 garlic clove, crushed
1 large carrot, coarsely grated
1–2 tbsp sunflower oil
1 tsp cumin seeds
2 tsp ground coriander
2 tsp black mustard seeds (optional)
4 cardamom pods
2 cups stock or water
1 bay leaf
salt and ground black pepper
½ cup unsalted nuts
fresh parsley or coriander, chopped,
　to garnish

1 Wash the rice either by the traditional Indian method (see below) or in a sieve under a running tap. If there is time, soak the rice for 30 minutes, then drain well in a sieve.

2 In a large shallow pan, gently fry the onion, garlic and carrot in the oil for a few minutes.

3 Stir in the rice and spices and cook for a further minute or two so that that the grains are coated in oil.

4 Pour in the stock or water, add the bay leaf and season well. Bring to a boil, cover and simmer very gently for about 10 minutes.

5 Remove from the heat without lifting the lid – this helps the rice to firm up and cook further. Leave for about 5 minutes.

6 If the rice is cooked, there will be small steam holes in the center. Discard the bay leaf and cardamom pods.

7 Stir in the nuts and check the seasoning. Scatter the mixture with the chopped parsley or coriander. This whole dish can be made ahead and reheated.

RINSING BASMATI

For light, fluffy grains basmati rice is best rinsed before cooking to remove any surface starch. The traditional method is to put the rice into a large bowl of cold water. Swill the grains around with your hands, then tip out the cloudy water. (The rice will quickly sink to the bottom). Repeat this action about five times. Ideally, leave the rice to soak for 30 minutes in the last rinsing water. This ensures a lighter, fluffier grain.

Quorn with Ginger, Chili and Leeks

Quorn is a newly-developed, versatile mycoprotein food which easily absorbs different flavors and retains a good firm texture. This makes it ideal for stir-frying. It is available in most supermarkets.

SERVES 4
8 oz Quorn cubes
3 tbsp soy sauce
2 tbsp dry sherry or vermouth
2 tsp honey
⅔ cup stock
2 tsp corn starch
3 tbsp sunflower or groundnut oil
3 leeks, thinly sliced
1 red chili, seeded and sliced
1 in piece fresh ginger root, peeled and shredded
salt and ground black pepper

1 Toss the Quorn in the soy sauce and sherry or vermouth until well coated and leave to marinate for about 30 minutes.

2 Strain the Quorn from the marinade and reserve the juices in a jug. Mix the marinade with the honey, stock and corn starch to make a paste.

3 Heat the oil in a wok or large frying pan and when hot, stir-fry the Quorn until it is crisp on the outside. Remove the Quorn and set aside.

4 Reheat the oil and stir-fry the leeks, chili and ginger for about 2 minutes until they are just soft. Season lightly.

5 Return the Quorn to the pan, together with the marinade, and stir well until the liquid is thick and glossy. Serve hot with rice or egg noodles.

Chinese Potatoes with Chili Beans

East meets West. An American style dish with a Chinese flavor – the sauce is particularly tasty. Try it as a quick supper dish when you fancy a meal with a little zing!

SERVES 4
4 medium potatoes, cut in thick chunks
3 scallions, sliced
1 large fresh chili, seeded and sliced
2 tbsp sunflower or groundnut oil
2 garlic cloves, crushed
1 × 14 oz can red kidney beans, drained
2 tbsp soy sauce
1 tbsp sesame oil
TO SERVE
salt and ground black pepper
1 tbsp sesame seeds
fresh coriander or parsley, chopped,
  to garnish

1 Boil the potatoes until they are just tender. Take care not to overcook them. Drain and reserve.

2 In a large frying pan or wok, stir-fry the scallions and chili in the oil for about 1 minute, then add the garlic and fry for a few seconds longer.

3 Add the potatoes, stirring well, then the beans and finally the soy sauce and sesame oil.

4 Season to taste and cook the vegetables until they are well heated through. Sprinkle with the sesame seeds and the coriander or parsley.

Tabbouleh

Almost the ultimate quick grain salad that simply needs soaking, draining and mixing. Bulgur is par boiled wheat. Make the salad a day ahead, if possible, so that the flavors have time to develop.

SERVES 4
¾ cup bulgur wheat
6 tbsp fresh lemon juice
5 tbsp extra virgin olive oil
6 tbsp fresh parsley, chopped
4 tbsp fresh mint, chopped
3 scallions, finely chopped
4 firm tomatoes, skinned and chopped
salt and ground black pepper

1 Cover the bulgur with cold water and soak for 20 minutes, then drain well and squeeze out even more water from it with your hands.

2 Put the bulgur into another bowl and add all the other ingredients, stirring and seasoning well.

3 Cover and chill for a few hours, or overnight, if possible.

Crudités with Humus

Always a great family favorite, home made humus is speedily produced with the help of a blender. The tahini paste is the secret of humus and it is readily available in delicatessens or larger supermarkets.

SERVES 2–3
1 × 15 oz can chick peas, drained
2 tbsp tahini paste
2 tbsp fresh lemon juice
1 garlic clove, crushed
salt and ground black pepper
olive oil and paprika pepper, to garnish
TO SERVE
Selection of salad vegetables, e.g. cucumber, chicory, baby carrots, pepper strips, radishes
Bite size chunks of bread, e.g. pitta, walnut, naan, bruschetta, or grissini sticks

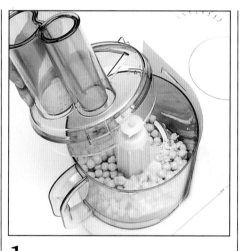

1 Put the chick peas, tahini paste, lemon juice, garlic and plenty of seasoning into a food processor or blender and mix to a smooth paste.

2 Spoon the humus into a bowl and swirl the top with the back of a spoon. Trickle over a little olive oil and sprinkle with paprika.

3 Prepare a selection of fresh salad vegetables and chunks of your favorite fresh bread or grissini sticks into finger size pieces.

4 Set out in a colorful jumble on a large plate with the bowl of humus in the center. Then dip and eat!

Pitta Pizzas

Pitta breads make very good bases for quick thin and crispy pizzas, and they are easy to eat with your hands too. The perfect speedy snack.

SERVES 4

EXTRA TOPPINGS – CHOOSE FROM
1 small red onion, thinly sliced and lightly fried
mushrooms, sliced and fried
1 × 7 oz can corn, drained
jalapeno chilis, sliced
black or green olives, pitted and sliced
capers, drained
BASIC PIZZAS
4 pitta breads, ideally whole wheat
small jar of pasta sauce
8 oz Mozzarella cheese, sliced or grated
dried oregano or thyme, to sprinkle
salt and ground black pepper

1 Prepare two or three toppings of your choice for the pizzas.

2 Preheat the broiler and lightly toast the pitta breads on each side.

3 Spread pasta sauce on each pitta, right to the edge. This prevents the edges of the pitta from burning.

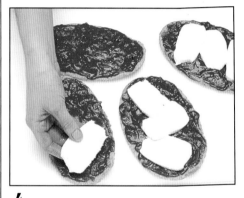

4 Arrange cheese slices or grated cheese on top of each pitta and sprinkle with herbs and seasoning.

5 Add the toppings of your choice and then broil the pizzas for about 5–8 minutes until they are golden brown and bubbling. Serve immediately.

Tagliatelle with Spinach and Soy Garlic Cheese

It's wonderful to mix ingredients from different cuisines and produce a delicious dish as a result. Italian pasta and spinach combine with Chinese soy and French garlic cream cheese to create this wonderful rich and mouth-watering dish.

SERVES 4

8 oz tagliatelle, preferably mixed colors
8 oz fresh leaf spinach, well washed
2 tbsp light soy sauce
3 oz carton garlic and herb cheese
3 tbsp milk
salt and ground black pepper

1 Boil the tagliatelle according to the instructions on the package and drain. Return the pasta to the pan.

2 Meanwhile blanch the spinach in a tiny amount of water until just wilted, then drain very well, squeezing dry with the back of a wooden spoon. Chop roughly with kitchen scissors.

3 Return the spinach to its pan and stir in the soy sauce, garlic and herb cheese and milk. Bring slowly to a boil, stirring until smooth. Season to taste.

4 When the sauce is ready, pour it over the pasta. Toss the pasta and sauce together well and serve hot.

Spaghetti with Feta

11·6 good

We think of pasta as being essentially Italian but, in fact, the Greeks have a great appetite for it too and it complements beautifully the tangy, full-flavored feta cheese.

SERVES 2
4 oz spaghetti
1 garlic clove
2 tbsp extra virgin olive oil
8 cherry tomatoes, halved
a little freshly grated nutmeg
salt and ground black pepper
3 oz feta cheese, crumbled
1 tbsp chopped fresh basil
a few black olives (optional), to serve

1 Boil the spaghetti in plenty of lightly salted water according to the instructions on the package, then drain.

2 In the same pan gently heat the garlic clove in the oil for a minute or two then add the cherry tomatoes.

3 Increase the heat to fry the tomatoes lightly for a minute, then remove the garlic and discard.

4 Toss in the spaghetti, add nutmeg and seasoning to taste and then stir in the crumbled feta and basil.

5 Check the seasoning, remembering that feta can be quite salty, and serve hot topped with olives if liked.

Potatoes with Blue Cheese and Walnuts

We are so used to eating potatoes as a side dish, we forget they can be a good main meal too. This dish is so versatile it can be served as either. Use Stilton, Danish Blue, Roquefort or any other blue veined cheese.

SERVES 4
1 lb small new potatoes
small head of celery, sliced
small red onion, sliced
4 oz blue cheese, mashed
⅔ cup light cream
salt and ground black pepper
½ cup walnut pieces
2 tbsp fresh parsley, chopped

1 Cover the potatoes with water and boil for about 15 minutes, adding the sliced celery and onion to the pan for the last 5 minutes or so.

2 Drain the vegetables and put them into a shallow serving dish.

3 In a small saucepan melt the cheese in the cream, slowly, stirring occasionally. Do not allow the mixture to boil but heat it until it scalds.

4 Season the sauce to taste. Pour it over the vegetables and scatter over the walnuts and parsley. Serve hot.

Aduki Bean Burgers

Although not quick to make, these burgers are a delicious alternative to store-bought ones; so it is worth making up several batches for the freezer. Use a long-grain brown rice, not a quick cook variety.

MAKES 12
1 cup brown rice
1 onion, chopped
2 garlic cloves, crushed
2 tbsp sunflower oil
4 tbsp butter
1 small green pepper, seeded and chopped
1 carrot, coarsely grated
1 × 14 oz can aduki beans, drained (or 4 oz dried weight, soaked and cooked)
1 egg, beaten
4 oz sharp cheese, grated
1 tsp dried thyme
½ cup roasted hazelnuts or toasted flaked almonds
salt and ground black pepper
whole wheat flour or cornmeal, for coating
oil, for deep frying

1 Cook the rice according to the instructions on the package, allowing it to slightly overcook so that it is softer. Strain the rice and transfer it to a large bowl.

2 Fry the onion and garlic in the oil and butter together with the green pepper and carrot for about 10 minutes until the vegetables are softened.

3 Mix this vegetable mixture into the rice, together with the aduki beans, egg, cheese, thyme, nuts or almonds and plenty of seasoning. Chill until quite firm.

4 Shape into 12 patties, using wet hands if the mixture sticks. Coat the patties in flour or cornmeal and set aside.

5 Heat ½ in oil in a large, shallow frying pan and fry the burgers in batches until browned on each side, about five minutes in total. Remove and drain on kitchen paper. Eat some burgers freshly cooked, and freeze the rest for later. Serve in buns with salad and relish.

COOK'S TIP

To freeze the burgers, cool them after cooking, then open freeze them before wrapping and bagging. Use within six weeks. Cook from frozen by baking in a pre-heated moderately hot oven for 20–25 minutes.

Zucchini Quiche 11-1 *Good*

If possible, use a hard goat cheese for this quiche as its flavor complements the zucchini nicely. Bake the pastry shell first for a crisp crust.

SERVES 6
PASTRY
scant 1 cup whole wheat flour
1 cup all-purpose flour
½ cup sunflower margarine
FILLING
1 red onion, thinly sliced
2 tbsp olive oil
2 large zucchini, sliced
6 oz cheese, grated
2 tbsp fresh basil, chopped
3 eggs, beaten
1¼ cups milk
salt and ground black pepper

1 Preheat the oven to 400°F. Mix the flours together and rub in the margarine until it resembles crumbs, then mix to a firm dough with cold water.

2 Roll out the pastry and use it to line a 9–10 in pie pan, ideally at least 1 in deep. Prick the base, chill for 30 minutes then fill with waxed paper or foil and baking beans.

3 Bake the pastry shell on a baking sheet for 20 minutes, uncovering it for the last 5 minutes so that it can crisp up.

4 Meanwhile, sweat the onion in the oil for 5 minutes, until it is soft. Add the zucchini and fry for another 5 minutes.

5 Spoon the onions and zucchini into the pastry case. Scatter over most of the cheese and all of the basil.

6 Beat together the eggs, milk and seasoning and pour over the filling. Top with the remaining cheese.

7 Turn the oven down to 350°F and return the quiche for about 40 minutes until risen and just firm to the touch in the center. Allow to cool slightly before serving.

MAIN COURSES

Create healthy and satisfying meals that make the most of the wonderful variety of herbs and spices, as well as nutritious ingredients such as lentils, rice and vegetables.

Arabian Spinach

Stir-fry spinach with onions and spices; then mix in a can of chick peas and you have a delicious family main course meal in next to no time.

SERVES 4
1 onion, sliced
2 tbsp olive or sunflower oil
2 garlic cloves, crushed
14 oz spinach, washed and shredded
1 tsp cumin seeds
1 × 15 oz can chick peas, drained
knob of butter
salt and ground black pepper

1 In a large frying pan or wok, fry the onion in the oil for about 5 minutes until softened. Add the garlic and cumin seeds, then fry for another minute.

2 Add the spinach, in stages, stirring it until the leaves begin to wilt. Fresh spinach condenses down dramatically on cooking and it *will* all fit into the pan.

3 Stir in the chick peas, butter and seasoning. Reheat until just bubbling, then serve hot. Drain off any pan juices, if you like, but this dish is rather nice served slightly saucy.

Vegetable Medley with Lentil Bolognese

Instead of a white or cheese sauce, it makes a nice change to top a selection of lightly steamed vegetables with a healthy and delicious lentil sauce.

SERVES 6
1 small cauliflower, in florets
8 oz broccoli florets
2 leeks, thickly sliced
8 oz Brussels sprouts, halved if large
Lentil Bolognese sauce

1 Make up the sauce and keep warm.

2 Place all the vegetables in a steamer over a pan of boiling water and cook for 8–10 minutes until just tender.

3 Drain and place in a shallow serving dish. Spoon the sauce on top, stirring slightly to mix. Serve hot.

Falafel 🌿

Made with ground chick peas, herbs and spices, falafel is a Middle Eastern street food normally served tucked into warm pitta breads with scoopfuls of salad. It is absolutely delicious served with tahini cream or dollops of natural yogurt.

MAKES 8
1 × 15 oz can chick peas, drained
1 garlic clove, crushed
2 tbsp fresh parsley, chopped
2 tbsp fresh coriander, chopped
1 tbsp fresh mint, chopped
1 tsp cumin seeds
2 tbsp fresh breadcrumbs
1 tsp salt
ground black pepper
oil, for deep frying

1 Grind the chick peas in a food processor until they are just smooth, then mix them with all the other ingredients until you have a thick, creamy paste. Add pepper to taste.

2 Using wet hands, shape the chick pea mixture into 8 balls and chill for 30 minutes so that they become firm.

3 Meanwhile, heat about ¼ in of oil in a shallow frying pan and fry the balls a few at a time. Cook each one for about 8 minutes, turning them all carefully just once.

4 Drain each ball on paper towel and fry the rest in batches, reheating the oil in between. Serve tucked inside warm pitta breads with sliced salad, tomatoes and tahini cream or yogurt.

COOK'S TIP

Falafel can be made in batches and frozen. Allow the balls to cool, spread out on wire racks and open freeze until solid. Tip into a freezer-proof plastic container. To reheat, bake in a moderate oven for 10–15 minutes.

Caribbean Rice and Peas 🌿

A great family favorite in West Indian culture, this dish is not only very tasty, but nutritionally well balanced too. Serve with slices of fried eggplant.

SERVES 4
1¼ cups quick cook unconverted long-grain rice
¾ cup dried gunga peas or red kidney beans, soaked and cooked but still firm
3⅔ cups water
2 oz creamed coconut, chopped
1 tsp dried thyme or 1 tbsp fresh thyme leaves
1 small onion stuck with 6 whole cloves
salt and ground black pepper

1 Put the rice and peas or kidney beans into a large saucepan with the water, coconut, thyme, onion and seasoning.

2 Bring to a boil, stirring until the coconut melts. Cover and simmer gently for 20 minutes.

3 Remove the lid and allow to cook uncovered for 5 minutes to reduce down any excess liquid. Remove from the heat and stir occasionally to separate the grains. The rice should be quite dry.

Greek Stuffed Vegetables 🌿

Vegetables such as peppers make wonderful containers for savory fillings. Instead of sticking to one type of vegetable, follow the Greeks' example and serve an interesting selection. Thick, creamy Greek yogurt is the ideal accompaniment.

SERVES 3–6
1 medium eggplant
1 large green pepper
2 large tomatoes
1 large onion, chopped
2 garlic cloves, crushed
3 tbsp olive oil
1 cup brown rice
2½ cups stock
¾ cup pine nuts
⅓ cup currants
salt and ground black pepper
3 tbsp fresh dill, chopped
3 tbsp fresh parsley, chopped
1 tbsp fresh mint, chopped
extra olive oil, to sprinkle
natural Greek yogurt, to serve
fresh sprigs of dill

1 Halve the eggplant, scoop out the flesh with a sharp knife and chop finely. Salt the insides and leave to drain upside down for 20 minutes while you prepare the other ingredients.

2 Halve the pepper, seed and core. Cut the tops from the tomatoes, scoop out the insides and chop roughly along with the tomato tops.

3 Fry the onion, garlic and chopped eggplant in the oil for 10 minutes, then stir in the rice and cook for 2 minutes.

4 Add the tomato flesh, stock, pine nuts, currants and seasoning. Bring to the boil, cover and simmer for 15 minutes then stir in the fresh herbs.

5 Blanch the eggplant and green pepper halves in boiling water for approximately 3 minutes, then drain them upside down.

6 Spoon the rice filling into all six vegetable "containers" and place on a lightly greased ovenproof shallow dish.

7 Heat the oven to 375°F, drizzle over some olive oil and bake the vegetables for 25–30 minutes. Serve hot, topped with spoonfuls of natural yogurt and dill sprigs.

Red Onion and Zucchini Pizza

It's easy to make a home made pizza using one of the new fast-action yeasts. You can either add the traditional cheese and tomato topping or try something different, such as the one described here.

SERVES 4
3 cups all-purpose flour
1 package fast action/easy blend yeast
2 tsp salt
lukewarm water to mix
TOPPING
2 red onions, thinly sliced
4 tbsp olive oil
2 zucchini, thinly sliced
salt and ground black pepper
fresh nutmeg, grated
4 oz semi-soft goat cheese
6 sun-dried tomatoes in oil, snipped
dried oregano
extra olive oil, to sprinkle

1 Preheat the oven to 400°F. Mix the flour, yeast and salt together, then mix to a firm dough with warm water. How much you will need depends on the flour, but start with ½ cup.

2 Knead the dough for about 5 minutes until it is smooth and elastic, then roll it out to a large circle and place on a lightly greased baking sheet.

3 Set the base aside somewhere warm to rise slightly while you make the topping.

4 Gently fry the onions in half the oil for 5 minutes then add the zucchini and fry for a further 2 minutes. Season and add nutmeg to taste.

5 Spread the pizza base with fried vegetable mixture and dot with the cheese, tomatoes and oregano. Sprinkle over the rest of the olive oil and bake for 12–15 minutes until golden and crisp.

Sprouting Beans and Pak Choi

Supermarkets are fast becoming cosmopolitan and many stock exotic varieties of vegetables.

SERVES 4
3 tbsp groundnut oil
3 scallions, sliced
2 garlic cloves, cut in slivers
1 in cube fresh ginger root ginger, cut in slivers
1 carrot, cut in thin sticks
5 oz sprouting beans (e.g. lentils, mung beans, chick peas)
1 × 7 oz pak choi cabbage, shredded
½ cup unsalted cashew nuts or halved almonds
SAUCE
3 tbsp light soy sauce
2 tbsp dry sherry
1 tbsp sesame oil
⅔ cup cold water
1 tsp corn starch
1 tsp honey
ground black pepper

1 Heat the oil in a large wok and stir-fry the onions, garlic, ginger and carrot for 2 minutes. Add the sprouting beans and fry for another 2 minutes, stirring and tossing them together.

2 Add the pak choi and nuts or almonds and stir-fry until the cabbage leaves are just wilting. Quickly mix all the sauce ingredients together in a jug and pour them into the wok, stirring immediately.

3 The vegetables will be coated in a thin, glossy sauce. Season and serve as soon as possible.

Thai Tofu Curry

Thai food is a marvelous mixture of Chinese and Indian styles, plus other delicious ingredients.

SERVES 4
2 × 7 oz packages tofu curd, cubed
2 tbsp light soy sauce
2 tbsp groundnut oil
PASTE
1 small onion, chopped
2 fresh green chilies, seeded and chopped
2 garlic cloves, chopped
1 tbsp grated fresh galingale or 1 tsp grated fresh ginger
2 kaffir lime leaves or 1 tsp lime rind, grated
2 tsp coriander berries, crushed
2 tsp cumin seeds, crushed
3 tbsp fresh coriander, chopped
1 tbsp Thai fish sauce (Nam pla) or soy sauce
juice of 1 lime or small lemon
1 tsp sugar
1 oz creamed coconut dissolved in ⅔ cup boiling water
GARNISH
thin slices fresh red chili or red pepper
fresh coriander leaves

1 Toss the tofu cubes in soy sauce and leave to marinate for 15 minutes or so while you prepare the paste.

2 Put all the paste ingredients into a food processor and grind until smooth.

3 To cook, heat the oil in a wok until quite hot. Drain the tofu cubes and stir-fry them at a high temperature until they are well browned on all sides and just firm. Drain on paper towel.

4 Wipe out the wok. Pour in the paste and stir well. Return the tofu to the wok and mix it into the paste, reheating the ingredients as you stir.

5 Serve this dish on a flat platter garnished with red chili or pepper and chopped coriander. Bowls of Thai fragrant or jasmine rice are the perfect accompaniment to the curry.

Festive Jalousie

An excellent puff pastry pie to serve either on Christmas Day or at anytime during the holiday period. Chinese dried chestnuts make an excellent substitute for fresh ones when soaked and cooked. Or you could drain a can of chestnuts.

SERVES 6
1 lb puff pastry, thawed if frozen
1 lb Brussels sprouts, trimmed
about 16 whole chestnuts, peeled if fresh
1 large red pepper, sliced
1 large onion, sliced
3 tbsp sunflower oil
1 large egg yolk, beaten with 1 tbsp
  water
SAUCE
scant ½ cup all-purpose flour
3 tbsp butter
½ pint milk
3 oz Cheddar cheese, grated
2 tbsp dry sherry
good pinch dried sage
salt and ground black pepper
3 tbsp fresh parsley, chopped

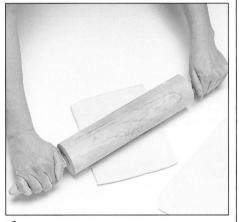

1 Roll out the pastry to make two large rectangles, roughly the size of your dish. The pastry should be about ¼ in thick and one rectangle should be slightly larger than the other. Set the pastry aside in the refrigerator.

2 Blanch the Brussels sprouts for 4 minutes in 1¼ cups boiling water, then drain them thoroughly, reserving the water. Refresh the sprouts under cold running water.

3 Cut each chestnut in half. Lightly fry the red pepper and onion in the oil for 5 minutes. Set aside till later.

4 Make up the sauce by beating the flour, butter and milk together over a medium heat. Beat the sauce continuously, bringing it to the boil, stirring until it is thickened and smooth.

5 Stir in the reserved sprout water, and the cheese, sherry, sage and seasoning. Simmer for 3 minutes to reduce and mix in the parsley.

6 Fit the larger piece of pastry into the pie dish and layer the sprouts, chestnuts, peppers and onions on top. Trickle over the sauce, making sure it seeps through to wet the vegetables.

7 Brush the pastry edges with beaten egg yolk and fit the second pastry sheet on top, pressing the edges well to seal them.

8 Crimp, press up the edges then mark the center. Glaze well all over with egg yolk. Set aside to rest somewhere cool while you preheat the oven to 400°F. Bake for 30–40 minutes until golden brown and crisp.

Shepherdess Pie

A no-meat version of the timeless classic, this dish also has no dairy products in it, so it is suitable for vegans. However, you can serve it with confidence to anyone wanting a hearty meal.

SERVES 6–8
2 lb potatoes
3 tbsp extra virgin olive oil
salt and ground black pepper
1 large onion, chopped
1 green pepper, chopped
2 carrots, coarsely grated
2 garlic cloves
3 tbsp sunflower oil or margarine
4 oz mushrooms, chopped
2 × 14 oz cans aduki beans, drained
2½ cups stock
1 tsp vegetable yeast extract
2 bay leaves
1 tsp dried mixed herbs
dried breadcrumbs or chopped nuts, to sprinkle

1 Boil the potatoes in the skins until tender, then drain, reserving a little of the water to moisten them.

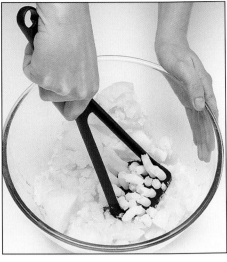

2 Peel the potatoes and mash them well, mixing in the olive oil and seasoning. (Potatoes are easier to peel when boiled in their skins. This also preserves vitamins.)

3 Gently fry the onion, pepper, carrots and garlic in the sunflower oil or margarine for about 5 minutes until they are soft.

4 Stir in the mushrooms and beans and cook for a further 2 minutes, then add the stock, yeast extract, bay leaves and mixed herbs. Simmer for 15 minutes.

5 Remove the bay leaves and empty the vegetables into a shallow ovenproof dish. Spoon on the potatoes in dollops and sprinkle over the crumbs or nuts. Broil until golden brown.

Magnificent Zucchini

At summer's end, large zucchini – with their wonderful green and cream stripes – look so attractive and tempting. They make delicious, inexpensive main courses, just right for a satisfying family Sunday lunch.

SERVES 4–6
3 cups pasta shells
3–4 lb zucchini
1 onion, chopped
1 pepper, seeded and chopped
1 tbsp fresh ginger root, grated
2 garlic cloves, crushed
3 tbsp sunflower oil
4 large tomatoes, skinned and chopped
salt and ground black pepper
½ cup pine nuts
1 tbsp fresh basil, chopped
cheese, grated, to serve (optional)

1 Preheat the oven to 375°F. Boil the pasta according to the instructions on the package, slightly overcooking it so that it is just a little soft. Drain thoroughly and set to one side.

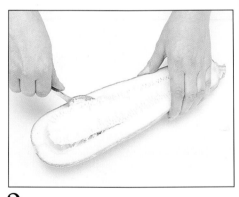

2 Cut the zucchini in half lengthwise and scoop out the seeds. These can be discarded. Use a small sharp knife and tablespoon to scoop out the zucchini flesh. Chop the flesh roughly.

3 Gently fry the onion, pepper, ginger and garlic in the oil for 5 minutes then add the zucchini flesh, tomatoes and seasoning. Cover and cook for 10–12 minutes until the vegetables are soft.

4 Add to the pan the pasta, pine nuts and basil, stir well and set aside.

5 Meanwhile, place the zucchini halves in a roasting pan, season lightly and pour a little water around the zucchini, taking care it does not spill inside. Cover with foil and bake for 15 minutes.

6 Remove the foil, discard the water and fill the shells with the vegetable mixture. Re-cover with foil and return to the oven for a further 20–25 minutes.

7 If you wish, serve this dish topped with grated cheese. The zucchini can either be served cut into sections or scooped out of the "shell."

Greek Spinach Pies

These little horns of filo pastry are stuffed with a simple spinach and feta cheese filling to make a quick and easy main course.

SERVES 8
8 oz fresh leaf spinach, well washed
2 scallions, chopped
6 oz feta cheese, crumbled
1 egg, beaten
1 tbsp fresh dill, chopped
ground black pepper
4 large sheets or 8 small sheets of
   filo pastry
olive oil, for brushing

COOK'S TIP

The pies can be prepared ahead and chilled for a day or two, before baking and serving warm. Alternatively, open freeze on a wire rack, then wrap well in foil or plastic wrap and freeze for up to one month. Uncover and thaw well before baking as the recipe above.

1 Preheat the oven to 375°F. Blanch the spinach in the tiniest amount of water until just wilted, then drain very well, pressing it through a sieve with the back of a wooden spoon.

2 Chop the spinach finely and mix with the onions, feta, egg, dill and ground black pepper.

3 Lay out a sheet of filo pastry and brush with olive oil. If large, cut the pieces in two and sandwich them together. If small, fit another sheet on top and brush with olive oil.

4 Spread a quarter of the filling on one edge of the filo at the bottom, then roll it up firmly, but not too tightly. Shape into a crescent and place on a baking sheet.

5 Brush the pastry well with oil and bake for about 20–25 minutes in the preheated oven until golden and crisp. Cool slightly then remove to a wire rack to cool further.

Chunky Vegetable Paella

This Spanish rice dish has become a firm family favorite the world over. There are very many versions: here is one with eggplant and chick peas.

SERVES 6
good pinch saffron strands
1 eggplant, cut in thick chunks
salt
6 tbsp olive oil
1 large onion, sliced
3 garlic cloves, crushed
1 yellow pepper, sliced
1 red pepper, sliced
2 tsp paprika
1¼ cups Arborio rice
2½ cups stock
1 lb fresh tomatoes, skinned and chopped
ground black pepper
4 oz sliced mushrooms
4 oz cut green beans
1 × 15 oz can chick peas

1 Steep the saffron in 3 tbsp hot water. Sprinkle the eggplant with salt, leave to drain in a colander for 30 minutes, then rinse and dry.

2 In a large paella or frying pan, heat the oil and fry the onion, garlic, peppers and eggplant for about 5 minutes, stirring occasionally. Sprinkle in the paprika and stir again.

3 Mix in the rice, then pour in the stock, tomatoes, saffron and seasoning. Bring to a boil then simmer for 15 minutes, uncovered, shaking the pan frequently and stirring occasionally.

4 Stir in the mushrooms, green beans and chick peas (with the liquor). Continue cooking for a further 10 minutes, then serve hot from the pan.

Green Lentil Kulbyaka

This traditional Russian dish, usually made with fish and dough, can be adapted to make a light, crisp vegetarian centerpiece using filo pastry and green lentils.

SERVES 6
1 cup green lentils, soaked for 30 minutes
2 bay leaves
2 onions, sliced
5 cups stock
¾ cup butter, melted
1¼ cups long grain rice, ideally basmati
salt and ground black pepper
4 tbsp fresh parsley, chopped
2 tbsp fresh dill, chopped
1 egg, beaten
8 oz mushrooms, sliced
about 8 sheets filo pastry
3 eggs, hard-boiled and sliced

1 Drain the lentils then simmer with the bay leaves, one onion and half the stock for 25 minutes until cooked and thick. Season well, cool and set aside.

VARIATION

You could use a vegetarian puff pastry. In this case, use two blocks of pastry, placing one on top of the other and rolling to a large rectangle. Alternatively, you could make two separate kulbyakas. Divide the filling between the pastry and seal the edges well, glazing the tops with beaten egg.

2 Gently fry the remaining onion in another saucepan with 2 tbsp of the butter for 5 minutes. Stir in the rice, then the rest of the stock.

3 Season, bring to the boil, then cover and cook gently for 12 minutes for basmati, 15 minutes for long grain. Leave to stand, uncovered, for 5 minutes, then stir in the fresh herbs. Cool, then beat in the raw egg.

4 Fry the mushrooms in 3 tbsp of the butter for 5 minutes until they are just soft. Cool and set aside.

5 Brush the inside of a large, shallow ovenproof dish with more butter. Lay the sheets of filo in it, covering the base and making sure most of the pastry overhangs the sides. Brush well with butter in between and overlapping the pastry as required. Ensure there is a lot of pastry to fold over the mounded filling.

6 Into the pastry lining, layer rice, lentils and mushrooms, repeating the layers at least once and tucking the sliced egg in between. Season as you layer and form an even mound of filling.

7 Bring up the sheets of pastry over the filling, scrunching the top into attractive folds. Brush all over with the rest of the butter and set aside to chill and firm up.

8 Preheat the oven to 375°F. When ready, bake the kulbyaka for about 45 minutes until golden and crisp. Allow to stand for 10 minutes before you cut it and serve.

Turnip and Chick Pea Cobbler

A good mid-week meal with an attractive savory scone topping. Use a star shape cutter for the topping.

SERVES 4–6
1 onion, sliced
2 carrots, chopped
3 medium size turnips, chopped
1 small sweet potato, chopped
2 celery stalks, sliced thinly
3 tbsp sunflower oil
½ tsp ground coriander
½ tsp dried mixed herbs
1 × 15 oz can chopped tomatoes
1 × 14 oz can chick peas
1 vegetable stock cube
salt and ground black pepper
TOPPING
2 cups self-rising flour
1 tsp baking powder
4 tbsp margarine
3 tbsp sunflower seeds
2 tbsp Parmesan cheese, grated
⅔ cup milk

1 Fry all the vegetables in the oil for about 10 minutes until they are soft. Add the coriander, herbs, tomatoes, chick peas with their liquor and stock cube. Season well and simmer for 20 minutes.

2 Pour the vegetables into a shallow casserole dish while you make the topping. Preheat the oven to 375°F.

3 Mix together the flour and baking powder, then rub in the margarine until it resembles fine crumbs. Stir in the seeds and Parmesan cheese. Add the milk and mix to a firm dough.

4 Lightly roll out the topping to a thickness of ½ in and stamp out star shapes or rounds, or simply cut it into small squares.

5 Place the shapes on top of the vegetable mixture and brush with a little extra milk. Bake for 12–15 minutes until risen and golden brown. Serve hot with green, leafy vegetables.

Tangy Fricassé

Vegetables in a light tangy sauce and covered with a crispy crumb topping make a simple and easy main course to serve with crusty bread and salad.

SERVES 4
4 zucchini, sliced
4 oz green beans, sliced
4 large tomatoes, skinned and sliced
1 onion, sliced
4 tbsp butter or sunflower margarine
⅓ cup all-purpose flour
2 tsp coarse grain mustard
2 cups milk
⅔ cup natural yogurt
1 tsp dried thyme
4 oz sharp cheese, grated
salt and ground black pepper
4 tbsp fresh whole wheat bread crumbs
  tossed with 1 tbsp sunflower oil

1 Blanch the zucchini and beans in a small amount of boiling water for just 5 minutes, then drain and arrange in a shallow ovenproof dish.

2 Arrange all but three slices of tomato on top. Put the onion into a saucepan with the butter or margarine and fry gently for 5 minutes.

3 Stir in the flour and mustard, cook for a minute then add the milk gradually until the sauce has thickened. Simmer for a further 2 minutes.

4 Remove the pan from the heat, add the yogurt, thyme and cheese, stirring until melted. Season to taste. Reheat gently if you wish, but do not allow the sauce to boil or it will curdle.

5 Pour the sauce over the vegetables and scatter the bread crumbs on top. Brown under a preheated broiler until golden and crisp, taking care not to let them burn. Garnish with the reserved tomato slices if desired.

Chili con Queso 🌿

Known as a "bowl of red," this classic Mexican dish is just as tasty when made with all-red beans. For an extra good flavor, use small cubes of smoked cheese, and serve with rice. Epazote is a traditional Mexican herb found in specialist stores.

SERVES 4
2 cups red kidney beans, soaked and drained
3 tbsp sunflower oil
1 onion, chopped
1 red pepper, chopped
2 garlic cloves, crushed
1 fresh red chili, chopped (optional)
1 tbsp chili powder (mild or hot)
1 tsp ground cumin
4 cups stock or water
1 tsp crushed dried epazote leaves (optional)
ground black pepper
salt
1 tsp granulated sugar
4 oz cheese, cubed, to serve

1 Rinse the beans. In a large saucepan heat the oil and gently fry the onion, pepper, garlic and fresh chili for about 5 minutes.

2 Stir in the spices and cook for another minute, then add the beans, stock or water, epazote (if using) and a grinding of pepper. Don't add salt at this stage.

3 Boil for 10 minutes, cover and turn down to a gentle simmer. Cook for about 50 minutes checking the water level and adding extra if necessary.

4 When the beans are tender, season them well with salt. Remove about a quarter of the mixture and mash to a pulp or pass through a food processor.

5 Return the purée to the pan and stir well. Add sugar and serve hot with the cheese sprinkled on top. Great with plain boiled long-grain rice.

Big Barley Bowl

Barley seems to have slipped from fashion in recent years – a pity as it is a delicious grain with a marvelous nutty texture. Serve this with crisp cheese croûtes.

SERVES 6
1 red onion, sliced
½ fennel bulb, sliced
2 carrots, cut in sticks
1 parsnip, sliced
3 tbsp sunflower oil
1 cup pearl barley
4 cups stock
1 tsp dried thyme
fresh parsley, chopped, to garnish
salt and ground black pepper
⅔ cup green beans, sliced
1 × 15 oz can pinto beans, drained
CROÛTES
1 medium sized baguette, sliced
olive oil, for brushing
1 garlic clove, cut in half
4 tbsp grated Parmesan cheese

1 In a large, heatproof casserole, sauté the onion, fennel, carrots and parsnip gently in the oil for 10 minutes.

2 Stir in the barley and stock. Bring to a boil, add the herbs and seasoning, then cover and simmer gently for 40 minutes.

3 Stir in the green beans and pinto beans and continue cooking – covered – for a further 20 minutes.

4 Meanwhile, preheat the oven to 375°F. Brush the baguette slices lightly with olive oil and then place them on a baking sheet.

5 Bake for about 15 minutes until light golden and crisp. Remove from the oven and quickly rub each croûte with the garlic halves. Sprinkle over the cheese and return to the oven to melt.

6 Ladle the barley into warm bowls and serve sprinkled with parsley, accompanied by the cheese croûtes. This dish is best eaten with a spoon.

Vegetables Julienne with Red Pepper Coulis

Just the right course for those watching their weight. Choose a selection of as many vegetables as you feel you can eat. Cut them into equal size finger lengths and steam them over aromatic, bubbling water.

SERVES 2

A selection of vegetables. Choose from: carrots, turnips, asparagus, parsnips, zucchini, green beans, broccoli, salsify, cauliflower, snow peas

RED PEPPER COULIS

1 small onion, chopped
1 garlic clove, crushed
1 tbsp sunflower oil
1 tbsp water
3 red peppers, roasted, skinned and chopped
8 tbsp low fat ricotta
squeeze of fresh lemon juice
salt and ground black pepper
sprigs of fresh thyme
2 bay leaves
fresh green herbs, to garnish

1 Prepare the vegetables by cutting them into thin fingers or small, even bite size pieces.

2 Make the coulis: lightly sauté the onion and garlic in the oil and water for 3 minutes then add the peppers and cook for a further 2 minutes.

3 Pass the coulis through a food processor, then work in the ricotta, lemon juice and seasoning.

4 Boil some salted water with the fresh thyme and bay leaves, and fit a steamer over the top.

5 Arrange the prepared vegetables on the steamer, placing the harder root vegetables at the bottom and steaming these for about 3 minutes.

6 Add the other vegetables according to their natural tenderness and cook for a further 2–4 minutes.

7 Serve the vegetables on plates with the sauce to one side. Garnish with fresh green herbs, if you wish.

VARIATION

The red pepper coulis makes a wonderful sauce for many other dishes. Try it spooned over fresh pasta with lightly steamed or fried zucchini, or use it as a pouring sauce for savory filled crêpes.

Pistachio Pilaf in a Spinach Crown

Saffron and ginger are traditional rice spices and even more delicious when mixed with fresh pistachio nuts. This is a particularly good, light main course needing just a tomato salad for accompaniment.

SERVES 4
3 onions
4 tbsp olive oil
2 garlic cloves, crushed
1 in cube fresh ginger root, grated
1 fresh green chili, chopped
2 carrots, coarsely grated
1¼ cups basmati rice, rinsed
¼ tsp saffron strands, crushed
2 cups stock
1 cinnamon stick
1 tsp ground coriander
salt and ground black pepper
¼ cup fresh pistachio nuts
1 lb fresh leaf spinach, well washed
1 tsp garam masala powder

1 Roughly chop two of the onions. Heat half the oil in a large saucepan and fry the onion with half the garlic, the ginger and the chili for 5 minutes.

2 Mix in the carrots and rice, cook for 1 more minute and then add the saffron, stock, cinnamon and coriander. Season well. Bring to a boil, then cover and simmer gently for 10 minutes, without lifting the lid.

3 Remove from the heat and leave to stand, uncovered, for 5 minutes. Add the pistachio nuts, mixing them in with a fork. Remove the cinnamon stick and keep the rice warm.

4 Thinly slice the third onion and fry in the remaining oil for about 3 minutes. Stir in the spinach. Cover and cook for another 2 minutes.

5 Add the garam masala powder. Cook until just tender then drain and roughly chop the spinach.

6 Spoon the spinach round the edge of a round serving dish and pile the pilaf in the center. Serve hot.

Spinach Bread and Butter Casserole

Ideally, use Italian ciabatta bread for this, or a French style baguette. It makes a much lighter dish.

SERVES 4–6
14 oz fresh leaf spinach
1 ciabatta loaf, thinly sliced
4 tbsp softened butter, olive oil or
   low fat spread
1 red onion, thinly sliced
4 oz mushrooms, thinly sliced
2 tbsp olive oil
1 tsp cumin seeds
salt and ground black pepper
4 oz Gruyère or Gouda cheese, grated
3 eggs
2¼ cups milk
fresh nutmeg, grated

1 Rinse the spinach well and blanch it in the tiniest amount of water for 2 minutes. Drain well, pressing out any excess water, and chop roughly.

2 Spread the bread slices thinly with the butter or low fat spread. Grease a large shallow ovenproof dish and line the base and sides with bread.

3 Fry the onion and mushrooms lightly in the oil for 5 minutes then add the cumin seeds and spinach. Season well.

4 Layer the spinach mixture with the remaining bread and half the cheese. For the top, mix everything together and sprinkle over the remaining cheese.

5 Beat the eggs with the milk, adding seasoning and nutmeg to taste. Pour slowly over the whole dish and set aside for a good hour to allow the custard to be absorbed into the bread.

6 Preheat the oven to 375°F. Stand the dish in a roasting pan and pour around some boiling water for a bain marie. Bake for 40–45 minutes until risen, golden brown and crispy on top.

Curried Parsnip Pie

Sweet, creamy parsnips are beautifully complemented by the addition of curry spices and cheese. This unusual but delicious combination of flavors makes for a very tasty pie.

SERVES 4

PASTRY
½ cup butter or margarine
1 cup all-purpose flour
salt and ground black pepper
1 tsp dried thyme or oregano
cold water, to mix

FILLING
8 baby onions, or shallots, peeled
2 large parsnips, thinly sliced
2 carrots, thinly sliced
2 tbsp butter or margarine
2 tbsp whole wheat flour
1 tbsp mild curry or tikka paste
1¼ cups milk
4 oz sharp cheese, grated
salt and ground black pepper
3 tbsp fresh coriander or parsley, chopped
1 egg yolk, beaten with 2 tsp water

1 Make the pastry by rubbing the butter or margarine into the flour until it resembles fine breadcrumbs. Season and stir in the thyme or oregano, then mix to a firm dough with cold water.

2 Blanch the baby onions or shallots with the parsnips and carrots in just enough water to cover, for about 5 minutes. Drain, reserving about 1¼ cups of the liquid.

3 In a clean pan, melt the butter or margarine, and stir in the flour and spice paste to make a roux. Gradually whisk in the reserved stock and milk until smooth. Simmer for a minute or two.

4 Take the pan off the heat, stir in the cheese and seasoning, then mix into the vegetables with the coriander or parsley.

COOK'S TIP

This pie freezes well and makes a good stand-by for a mid-week meal. For best results, make up to the final stage and freeze unbaked. Open freeze until solid, then wrap well in freezer plastic wrap, seal and label. Use within one month.

Cauliflower, broccoli or any other favorite vegetable can be added to the filling to give a variety of flavors and textures.

5 Pour into a pie dish, fix a pie funnel in the center and allow to cool.

6 Roll out the pastry, large enough to fit the top of the pie dish. Re-roll the trimmings into long strips.

7 Brush the pastry edges with egg yolk wash and fit on the pastry strips. Brush again with egg yolk wash.

8 Using a rolling pin, lift the rolled out pastry over the pie top and fit over the funnel, pressing it down well onto the strips underneath.

9 Cut off the overhanging pastry and crimp the edges. Cut a hole for the funnel, brush all over well with the remaining egg yolk wash and make decorations with the trimmings, glazing them too.

10 Place the pie dish on a baking sheet and chill for 30 minutes while you preheat the oven to 400°F. Bake the pie for about 25–30 minutes until golden brown and crisp on top.

4 1/2★ Excellent - this came out really good, easy to make, tasty. I would make again. Great for meatless Mon.!

Vegetables under a Light Creamy Crust

This light main course dish is ideal for a summer supper. The subtle flavors of leeks, zucchini and mushrooms are topped by a tasty crust of ricotta, Parmesan cheese and bread crumbs.

SERVES 4
2 leeks, thinly sliced *onions*
3 zucchini, thickly sliced
12 oz sliced mushrooms, including oyster and shiitake mushrooms *I added sliced carrots*
2 garlic cloves, crushed *- brussel sprouts*
2 tbsp olive oil *- string beans*
2 tbsp butter *the more veggies*
spelt → 1 tbsp all-purpose <u>flour</u> *the better!*
1¼ cups stock *1c.*
1 tsp dried thyme
salt and ground black pepper
2 tbsp ricotta cheese
TOPPING
1 lb ricotta cheese
2 tbsp butter, melted
3 eggs, beaten
salt and ground black pepper
fresh nutmeg, grated
freshly grated Parmesan cheese and
~~dried bread crumbs, to sprinkle~~

increase to 375° at end to brown top.

1 Preheat the oven to 375°F. *350°* In a saucepan, gently fry the leeks, zucchini, mushrooms and garlic in the oil and butter for about 7 minutes, stirring occasionally, until the vegetables are just soft.

2 Stir in the flour, then gradually mix in the stock. Bring to a boil, stirring until thickened. Add the thyme and seasoning. Take the pan off the heat and stir in the ricotta. Pour the vegetable mixture into a shallow ovenproof dish.

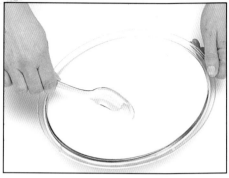

3 Beat the topping ingredients together, seasoning them well and adding the nutmeg to taste. Spoon on top of the vegetables and sprinkle with Parmesan cheese and bread crumbs.

4 Bake for about 30 minutes until a light golden, firm crust forms. Serve hot with pasta or crusty bread.

Potato and Parsnip Amandine

Shells of baked potatoes are filled with a spicy parsnip and crunchy almond mix. They make an unusual alternative to plain baked potatoes.

SERVES 4
4 large baking potatoes
olive oil, for greasing
8 oz parsnips, diced
2 tbsp butter
1 tsp cumin seeds
1 tsp ground coriander
2 tbsp light cream or natural yogurt
salt and ground black pepper
4 oz Gruyère or Cheddar cheese, grated
1 egg, beaten
¼ cup flaked almonds

1 Rub the potatoes all over with oil, score in half, then bake at 400°F for about 1 hour until cooked.

2 Meanwhile, boil the parsnips until tender, then drain well, mash and mix with the butter, spices and cream or natural yogurt.

3 When the potatoes are cooked, halve, scoop out and mash the flesh then mix with the parsnip, seasoning well.

4 Stir in the cheese, egg and three quarters of the almonds. Fill the potato shells with the mixture and sprinkle over the remaining almonds.

5 Return to the oven and bake for about 15–20 minutes until golden brown and the filling has set lightly. Serve hot with a side salad.

Baked Pumpkin

Glorious pumpkin shells evoke the delights of the fall season and seem too good simply to throw away. Use one instead as a serving pot. Pumpkin and pasta make marvelous partners, especially as a main course served from the baked shell.

SERVES 4
1 × 4 lb pumpkin
1 onion, sliced
1 in cube fresh ginger root
3 tbsp extra virgin olive oil
1 zucchini, sliced
4 oz sliced mushrooms
1 × 14 oz can chopped tomatoes
1 cup pasta shells
2 cups stock
salt and ground black pepper
4 tbsp ricotta cheese
2 tbsp fresh basil, chopped

1 Preheat the oven to 350°F. Cut the top off the pumpkin with a large, sharp knife, then scoop out and discard all the seeds.

2 Using a small, sharp knife and a sturdy tablespoon extract as much of the pumpkin flesh as possible, then chop it into chunks.

3 Bake the pumpkin with its lid on for 45 minutes to one hour until the inside begins to soften.

4 Meanwhile, make the filling. Gently fry the onion, ginger and pumpkin flesh in the olive oil for about 10 minutes, stirring occasionally.

5 Add the zucchini and mushrooms and cook for a further 3 minutes, then stir in the tomatoes, pasta shells and stock. Season well, bring to a boil, then cover and simmer gently for 10 minutes.

6 Stir the ricotta cheese and basil into the pasta and spoon the mixture into the pumpkin. It may not be possible to fit all the filling into the pumpkin shell, so serve the rest separately if this is the case.

Festive Lentil and Nut Roast

An excellent celebration dish which can be served with all the trimmings, including vegetarian gravy. Garnish it with fresh cranberries and French parsley for a really festive effect.

SERVES 6–8
⅔ cup red lentils
1 cup hazelnuts
1 cup walnuts
1 large carrot
2 celery stalks
1 large onion
4 oz mushrooms
4 tbsp butter
2 tsp mild curry powder
2 tbsp tomato ketchup
2 tbsp Worcestershire sauce
1 egg, beaten
2 tsp salt
4 tbsp fresh parsley, chopped
⅔ cup water

1 Soak the lentils for 1 hour in cold water then drain well. Grind the nuts in a food processor until quite fine but not too smooth. Set the nuts aside.

2 Chop the carrot, celery, onion and mushrooms into small chunks, then pass them through a food processor or blender until they are quite finely chopped.

3 Fry the vegetables gently in the butter for 5 minutes, then stir in the curry powder and cook for a minute. Cool.

4 Meanwhile, mix the soaked lentils with the nuts, vegetables, ketchup, Worcestershire sauce, egg, salt, parsley and water.

5 Grease and line the base and sides of a long 2 lb loaf pan with waxed paper or a sheet of foil. Press the mixture firmly into the pan and smooth the surface. Preheat the oven to 375°F.

6 Bake for about 1–1¼ hours until just firm, covering the top with a butter paper or piece of foil if it starts to burn.

7 Allow the mixture to stand for about 15 minutes before you turn it out and peel off the paper. It will be fairly soft when cut as it is a moist loaf.

Vegetarian Gravy

Make up a large batch of this and freeze it in small containers ready to reheat and serve. A delicious alternative to the meat version.

MAKES ABOUT 1¾ PINTS
1 large red onion, sliced
3 turnips, sliced
3 celery stalks, sliced
4 oz mushrooms, halved
2 whole garlic cloves
6 tbsp sunflower oil
6 cups vegetable stock or water
3 tbsp soy sauce
good pinch of granulated sugar
salt and ground black pepper

1 Cook the vegetables and garlic on a moderately high heat with the oil in a large saucepan, stirring occasionally until nicely browned but not singed. This should take about 15–20 minutes.

2 Add the stock or water and soy sauce and bring to a boil, then cover and simmer for another 20 minutes.

3 Purée the vegetables, adding a little of the stock, and return them to the pan by rubbing the pulp through a sieve with the back of a ladle or wooden spoon.

4 Taste for seasoning and add the sugar. Freeze at least half of the gravy to use later and reheat the rest to serve with the lentil and nut roast.

Homemade Ravioli

It is a pleasure to make your own fresh pasta and you might be surprised at just how easy it is to fill and shape ravioli. Allow a little extra time than you would for ready-made or dried pasta. A food processor will save you time and effort in making and kneading the dough. A pasta rolling machine helps with the rolling out, but both these jobs can be done by hand if necessary.

SERVES 6
1½ cups all-purpose flour
½ tsp salt
1 tbsp olive oil
2 eggs, beaten
FILLING
1 small red onion, finely chopped
1 small green pepper, finely chopped
1 carrot, coarsely grated
1 tbsp olive oil
½ cup walnuts, chopped
4 oz ricotta cheese
2 tbsp fresh Parmesan or Pecorino cheese, grated
1 tbsp fresh marjoram or basil, chopped
salt and ground black pepper
extra oil or melted butter, to serve

1 Sift the flour and salt into a food processor. With the machine running, trickle in the oil and eggs and blend to a stiff but smooth dough.

2 Allow the machine to run for at least a minute if possible, otherwise remove the dough and knead it by hand for 5 minutes.

3 If using a pasta machine, break off small balls of dough and then feed them through the rollers a number of times, according to the manufacturer's instructions.

4 If rolling the pasta by hand, divide the dough into two. With a rolling pin roll out on a lightly floured surface to a thickness of about ¼ in.

5 Fold the pasta into three and re-roll. Repeat this up to six times until the dough is smooth and no longer sticky. Roll the pasta a little more thinly each time.

6 Keep the rolled dough under clean, dry dish towels while you complete the rest and make the filling. You should aim to have an even number of pasta sheets, all the same size if rolling by machine.

7 Fry the onion, pepper and carrot in the oil for 5 minutes, then allow to cool. Mix with the walnuts, cheeses, herbs and seasoning.

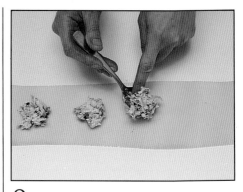

8 Lay out a pasta sheet and place small scoops of the filling in neat rows about 2 in apart. Brush in between with a little water and then place another pasta sheet on the top.

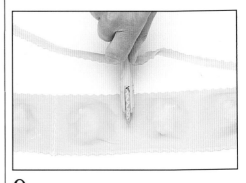

9 Press down well in between the rows then, using a ravioli or pastry cutter, cut into squares. If the edges pop open occasionally, press them back gently with your fingers.

10 Leave the ravioli to dry in the refrigerator, then boil in plenty of lightly salted water for just 5 minutes.

11 Toss the cooked ravioli in a little oil or melted butter before serving with either home made tomato sauce or some extra cheese.

Mushroom Puffs

If possible, use the fuller-flavored cremini, or brown, mushrooms for these tasty puffs.

MAKES 8
2 × 8 oz blocks frozen puff pastry, thawed
1 egg, beaten
FILLING
1 onion, chopped
1 carrot, coarsely grated
1 medium potato, coarsely grated
3 tbsp sunflower oil
8 oz sliced mushrooms
2 tbsp soy sauce
1 tbsp tomato ketchup
1 tbsp dry sherry (optional)
good pinch dried thyme
salt and ground black pepper

1 Roll out the pastry blocks until they are ¼ in thick and cut each block into four 6 in squares. Reserve a little pastry for decoration. Cover the rolled pastry squares and trimmings and set aside in a cool place to rest.

2 Make the filling by gently frying the onion, carrot and potato in the oil for 5 minutes, then add the mushrooms, soy sauce, ketchup, sherry (if using), thyme and seasoning.

3 Cook, stirring occasionally, until the mushrooms and vegetables have softened and feel quite tender. Cool.

4 Divide the filling between the eight squares, placing it to one side across the diagonal. Brush the pastry edges with egg then fold over into triangles and press well to seal. From the pastry scraps, cut out little shapes, such as mushrooms, to decorate the pasties.

5 Crimp each puff edge and top with the cut-out shapes. Set on two baking sheets. Preheat the oven to 400°F and, in the meantime, allow the puffs to rest somewhere cool.

6 Glaze the puffs with beaten egg, then bake for 15–20 minutes until golden brown and crisp.

Winter Casserole with Herb Dumplings

When the cold weather draws in, gather together a good selection of vegetables and make this comforting casserole with some hearty old-fashioned dumplings.

SERVES 6
2 potatoes
2 carrots
1 small fennel bulb
1 small rutabaga
2 leeks
2 zucchini
4 tbsp butter or margarine
2 tbsp all-purpose flour
1 × 15 oz can lima beans, with liquor
2½ cups stock
2 tbsp tomato paste
1 cinnamon stick
2 tsp ground coriander
½ tsp ground ginger
2 bay leaves
salt and ground black pepper
DUMPLINGS
1½ cups all-purpose flour
4 oz vegetable suet, shredded, or chilled
    butter, grated
1 tsp dried thyme
1 tsp salt
½ cup milk

1 Cut all the vegetables into even, bite size chunks, then fry gently in the butter or margarine for about 10 minutes.

2 Stir in the flour then the liquor from the beans, the stock, tomato paste, spices, bay leaves and seasoning. Bring to a boil, stirring all the time.

3 Cover and simmer for 10 minutes, then add the beans and cook for a further 5 minutes.

4 Meanwhile, to make the dumplings, simply mix the flour, suet or butter, thyme and salt to a firm but moist dough with the milk and knead with your hands until it is smooth.

VARIATION

Try chopped walnuts and grated Parmesan or dumplings *fines herbes*. Finely chop ingredients and stir into flour.

5 Divide the dough into 12 pieces, rolling each one into a ball with your fingers. Uncover the simmering stew and then add the dumplings, allowing space between each one for expansion.

6 Replace the lid and cook on a gentle simmer for a further 15 minutes. Do not peek – or you will let out all the steam. Neither should you cook dumplings too fast, or they will break up. Remove the cinnamon stick and bay leaves before you serve this dish, steaming hot.

Lasagne Rolls

Perhaps a more elegant presentation than ordinary lasagne, but just as tasty and popular. You will need to boil "no-need-to-cook" lasagne as it needs to be soft enough to roll!

SERVES 4
8–10 lasagne sheets
Lentil Bolognese (see below)
8 oz fresh leaf spinach, well washed
4 oz mushrooms, sliced
4 oz Mozzarella cheese, thinly sliced
BECHAMEL SAUCE
scant ½ cup all-purpose flour
3 tbsp butter or margarine
2½ cups milk
bay leaf
salt and ground black pepper
fresh nutmeg, grated
freshly grated Parmesan or Pecorino
  cheese, to serve

Lentil Bolognese

A really useful sauce to serve with pasta, such as lasagne rolls, as a crêpe stuffing or even as a protein-packed sauce for vegetables.

SERVES 6
1 onion, chopped
2 garlic cloves, crushed
2 carrots, coarsely grated
2 celery stalks, chopped
3 tbsp olive oil
⅔ cup red lentils
1 × 14 oz can chopped tomatoes
2 tbsp tomato paste
2 cups stock
1 tbsp fresh marjoram, chopped, or
  1 tsp dried marjoram
salt and ground black pepper

1 Cook the lasagne sheets according to instructions on the package, or for about 10 minutes. Drain and allow to cool.

2 Cook the spinach in the tiniest amount of water for 2 minutes then add the sliced mushrooms and cook for a further 2 minutes. Drain very well, pressing out all the excess liquor, and chop roughly.

3 Put all the bechamel ingredients into a saucepan and bring slowly to a boil, stirring continuously until the sauce is thick and smooth. Simmer for 2 minutes with the bay leaf then season well and stir in grated nutmeg to taste.

VARIATION

Needless to say, the fillings in this recipe could be any of your own choice. One of my favorites is a lightly stir-fried mixture of colorful vegetables such as peppers, zucchini, eggplant and mushrooms, topped with a cheese bechamel as above, or with a fresh tomato sauce, which is especially good in summer.

4 Lay out the pasta sheets and spread with the bolognese sauce, spinach and mushrooms and mozzarella. Roll up each one and place in a large shallow casserole dish with the join face down.

5 Remove and discard the bay leaf and then pour the sauce over the pasta. Sprinkle over the cheese and place under a hot broiler to brown.

1 In a large saucepan, gently fry the onion, garlic, carrots and celery in the oil for about 5 minutes, until they are soft.

2 Add the lentils, tomatoes, tomato paste, stock, marjoram and seasoning.

3 Bring the mixture to a boil then partially cover with a lid and simmer for 20 minutes until thick and soft. Use the bolognese sauce as required.

Artichoke and Leek Crêpes

Fill wafer-thin crêpes with a mouth-watering soufflé mixture of Jerusalem artichokes and leek to serve for a special main course.

SERVES 4
1 cup all-purpose flour
pinch of salt
1 egg
1¼ cups milk
oil, for brushing
SOUFFLÉ FILLING
1 lb Jerusalem artichokes, peeled and diced
1 large leek, sliced thinly
4 tbsp butter
2 tbsp self-rising flour
2 tbsp light cream
3 oz sharp Cheddar cheese, grated
2 tbsp fresh parsley, chopped
fresh nutmeg, grated
2 eggs, separated
salt and ground black pepper

2 Using a crêpe or omelette pan with a diameter of about 8 in, make a batch of thin pancakes. You will need about 2 tbsp of batter for each one.

3 Stack the pancakes under a clean dish towel as you make them. Reserve eight for this dish and freeze the rest.

4 Cook the artichokes and leek with the butter in a covered saucepan on a gentle heat for about 12 minutes until very soft. Mash with the back of a wooden spoon. Season well.

5 Stir the flour into the vegetables and cook for 1 minute. Take the pan off the heat and beat in the cream, cheese, parsley and nutmeg to taste. Cool, then add the egg yolks.

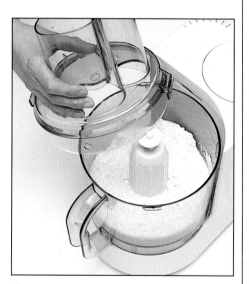

1 Make the crêpe batter by blending the flour, salt, egg and milk to a smooth batter in a food processor or blender.

6 Whisk the egg whites until they form soft peaks and carefully fold them into the leek/artichoke mixture.

7 Lightly grease a small ovenproof dish and preheat the oven to 375°F. Fold each pancake in four, hold the top open and then carefully spoon the filling mixture into the center.

8 Arrange the crêpes in the prepared dish with the filling uppermost if possible. Bake for about 15 minutes until risen and golden. Eat immediately!

COOK'S TIP

Make sure the pan is at a good steady heat and is well oiled before you pour in the batter. It should sizzle as it hits the pan. Swirl the batter round to coat the pan, and then cook quickly.

2-19-96 Good

Broccoli Risotto Torte

Like a Spanish omelette, this is a savory cake served in wedges. It is good cold or hot, and needs only a salad as an accompaniment.

SERVES 6

8 oz broccoli, cut into very small florets
1 onion, chopped
2 garlic cloves, crushed
1 large yellow pepper, sliced
2 tbsp olive oil
4 tbsp butter
1¼ cups Arborio rice
½ cup dry white wine
4½ cups stock
salt and ground black pepper
4 oz fresh or Parmesan cheese, coarsely
   grated
4 eggs, separated
oil, for greasing
sliced tomato and chopped parsley,
   to garnish

---

1 Blanch the broccoli for 3 then drain and reserve.

2 In a large saucepan, gentl onion, garlic and pepper in the oil and butter for 5 minutes until they are soft.

3 Stir in the rice, cook for a minute then pour in the wine. Cook, stirring the mixture until the liquid is absorbed.

4 Pour in the stock, season well, bring to a boil then lower to a simmer. Cook for 20 minutes, stirring occasionally.

while, grease a 10 in round pan and then line the base of waxed paper. Preheat the 0°F.

6 Stir the cheese into the rice, allow the mixture to cool for 5 minutes, then beat in the egg yolks.

7 Whisk the egg whites until they form soft peaks and carefully fold into the rice. Turn into the prepared pan and bake for about 1 hour until risen, golden brown and slightly wobbly in the center.

8 Allow the torte to cool in the pan, then chill if serving cold. Run a knife round the edge of the pan and shake out onto a serving plate. If liked, garnish with sliced tomato and chopped parsley.

Leek and Chèvre Lasagne

An unusual and lighter than average lasagne using a soft French goat cheese. The pasta sheets are not so chewy if boiled briefly first. If you do choose no-cook lasagne, then make more sauce to soak into the pasta.

SERVES 6
6–8 lasagne pasta sheets
salt
1 large eggplant
3 leeks, thinly sliced
2 tbsp olive oil
2 red peppers, roasted
7 oz Chèvre, broken into pieces
2 oz Pecorino or Parmesan cheese, freshly
  grated
SAUCE
½ cup all-purpose flour
5 tbsp butter
3¾ cups milk
½ tsp ground bay leaves
fresh nutmeg, grated
ground black pepper

1 Blanch the pasta sheets in plenty of boiling water for just 2 minutes. Drain and place on a clean dish towel.

2 Lightly salt the eggplant and lay in a colander to drain for 30 minutes, then rinse and pat dry with paper towel.

3 Lightly fry the leeks in the oil for about 5 minutes until softened. Peel the roasted peppers and cut into strips.

4 Make the sauce: put the flour, butter and milk into a saucepan and bring to a boil, stirring constantly until it has thickened. Add the ground bay leaves, nutmeg and seasoning. Simmer for a further 2 minutes.

5 In a greased shallow casserole, layer the leeks, pasta, eggplant, Chèvre and Pecorino or Parmesan. Trickle the sauce over the layers, ensuring that plenty goes in between.

6 Finish with a layer of sauce and grated cheese. Bake in the oven at 375°F for 30 minutes or until browned on top. Serve the lasagne immediately.

Glamorgan Sausages

An old Welsh recipe which tastes particularly good served with creamy mashed potatoes and lightly cooked green cabbage.

SERVES 4
2 cups fresh whole wheat bread crumbs
6 oz sharp Cheddar or Caerphilly
  cheese, grated
2 tbsp leek or scallion, finely chopped
2 tbsp fresh parsley, chopped
1 tbsp fresh marjoram, chopped
1 tbsp coarse grain mustard
2 eggs, 1 separated
ground black pepper
½ cup dried bread crumbs
oil, for deep fat frying

1 Mix the fresh bread crumbs with the cheese, leek or scallion, parsley, marjoram, mustard, whole egg, one egg yolk and black pepper to taste. The mixture may appear dry at first but if you knead it lightly it will come together. Make 8 small sausage shapes.

2 Whisk the egg white until lightly frothy and put the dried bread crumbs into a bowl. Dip the sausages first into egg white, and then coat them evenly in breadcrumbs, shaking off any excess.

3 Heat a deep fat frying pan a third full of oil and carefully fry four sausages at a time for 2 minutes each. Drain on paper towel and reheat the oil to repeat.

4 Keep the sausages warm in the oven, uncovered. Alternatively, open freeze, bag and seal, then to reheat, thaw for 1 hour and cook in a moderately hot oven for 10–15 minutes.

Brazilian Stuffed Peppers

Colorful and full of flavor, these stuffed peppers are easy to make in advance. They can be reheated quickly in a microwave oven and browned under a broiler.

SERVES 4
4 peppers, halved and seeded
1 eggplant, cut in chunks
1 onion, sliced
1 garlic clove, crushed
2 tbsp olive oil
1 × 14 oz can chopped tomatoes
1 tsp ground coriander
salt and ground black pepper
1 tbsp fresh basil, chopped
4 oz goat cheese, coarsely crumbled
2 tbsp dried bread crumbs

1 Blanch the pepper halves in boiling water for 3 minutes, then drain well.

2 Sprinkle the eggplant chunks with salt, place in a colander and leave to drain for 20 minutes. Rinse and pat dry.

3 Fry the onion and garlic in the oil for 5 minutes until they are soft, then add the eggplant and cook for a further 5 minutes, stirring occasionally.

VARIATION

There are all sorts of delicious stuffings for peppers. Rice or pasta make a good base, mixed with some lightly fried onion, garlic and spices. Mixed nuts, finely chopped, can be added and a beaten egg or grated cheese helps to bind it all together. Vegans can leave out the last two ingredients.

4 Pour in the tomatoes, coriander and seasoning. Bring to a boil, then simmer for 10 minutes until the mixture is thick. Cool slightly, stir in the basil and half of the cheese.

5 Spoon into the pepper halves and place on a shallow heatproof serving dish. Sprinkle with cheese and bread crumbs, then brown lightly under the broiler. Serve with rice and salad.

Mushroom Gougère *add more veggies!*

A savory choux pastry ring makes a marvelous main course dish that can be made ahead then baked when required. Why not try it for a dinner party? It looks so very special.

SERVES 4
½ cup all-purpose flour
½ tsp salt
6 tbsp butter
¾ cup cold water
3 eggs, beaten
¾ cup diced Gruyère or aged Gouda
  cheese
FILLING
1 small onion, sliced
1 carrot, coarsely grated
8 oz button mushrooms, sliced
3 tbsp butter or margarine
1 tsp tikka or mild curry paste
2 tbsp all-purpose flour
1¼ cups milk
2 tbsp fresh parsley, chopped
salt and ground black pepper
2 tbsp flaked almonds

1 Preheat the oven to 400°F. Grease a shallow ovenproof dish approximately 9 in long.

2 To make the choux pastry, first sift the flour and salt onto a large sheet of waxed paper.

3 In a large saucepan, heat the butter and water until the butter just melts. Do not let the water boil. Fold the paper and shoot the flour into the pan all at once.

4 With a wooden spoon, beat the mixture rapidly until the lumps become smooth and the mixture comes away from the sides of the pan. Cool for 10 minutes.

5 Beat the eggs gradually into the mixture until you have a soft, but still quite stiff, dropping consistency. You may not need all the egg.

6 Stir in the cheese, then spoon the mixture round the sides of the greased ovenproof dish.

7 To make the filling, sauté the onion, carrot and mushrooms in the butter or margarine for 5 minutes. Stir in the curry paste then the flour.

8 Gradually stir in the milk and heat until thickened. Mix in the parsley, season well, then pour into the center of the choux pastry.

9 Bake for 35–40 minutes until risen and golden brown, sprinkling on the almonds for the last 5 minutes or so. Serve at once.

COOK'S TIP

Choux pastry is remarkably easy to make, as no rolling out is required. The secret of success is to let the flour and butter mixture cool before beating in the eggs, to prevent them from setting.

Couscous-stuffed Cabbage

A whole stuffed cabbage makes a wonderful main dish, especially for a Sunday lunch. It can be made ahead and steamed when required. Cut into wedges and serve accompanied by a fresh tomato or cheese sauce or even a vegetarian gravy.

SERVES 4
1 medium size cabbage
1 cup couscous grains
1 onion, chopped
1 small red pepper, chopped
2 garlic cloves, crushed
2 tbsp olive oil
1 tsp ground coriander
½ tsp ground cumin
good pinch ground cinnamon
½ cup green lentils, soaked
2½ cups stock
2 tbsp tomato paste
salt and ground black pepper
2 tbsp fresh parsley, chopped
2 tbsp pine nuts or flaked almonds
3 oz sharp Cheddar cheese, grated
1 egg, beaten

1 Cut the top quarter off the cabbage and remove any loose outer leaves. Using a small sharp knife, cut out as much of the middle as you can. Reserve a few larger leaves for later.

2 Blanch the cabbage in a pan of boiling water for 5 minutes, then drain it well, upside down.

VARIATION

You could substitute healthy brown rice for the couscous.

3 Steam the couscous according to the instructions on the package, ensuring that the grains are light and fluffy.

4 Lightly fry the onion, pepper and garlic in the oil for 5 minutes until soft then stir in the spices and cook for a further 2 minutes.

5 Add the lentils and pour in the stock and tomato paste. Bring to a boil, season and simmer for 25 minutes until the lentils are cooked.

6 Mix in the couscous, parsley, nuts or almonds, cheese and egg. Check the seasoning again. Open up the cabbage and spoon in the stuffing.

7 Blanch the leftover outer cabbage leaves and place these over the top of the stuffing, then wrap the whole cabbage in a sheet of buttered foil.

8 Place in a steamer over simmering water and cook for about 45 minutes. Remove from the foil and serve cut into wedges.

Couscous Aromatique

The cuisine of Morocco and Tunisia has many wonderful dishes using the wheat grain couscous which is steamed over simmering spicy stews. A little of the fiery harissa paste stirred in at the end adds an extra zing.

SERVES 4–6
1 lb couscous grains
4 tbsp olive oil
1 onion, cut in chunks
2 carrots, cut in thick slices
4 baby turnips, halved
8 small new potatoes, halved
1 green pepper, cut in chunks
4 oz green beans, halved
1 small fennel bulb, sliced thickly
1 in cube fresh ginger root, grated
2 garlic cloves, crushed
1 tsp ground turmeric
1 tbsp ground coriander
1 tsp cumin seeds
1 tsp ground cinnamon
3 tbsp red lentils
1 × 14 oz can chopped tomatoes
4½ cups stock
4 tbsp raisins
salt and ground black pepper
rind and juice of 1 lemon
harissa paste, to serve (optional)

1 Cover the couscous with cold water and soak for 10 minutes. Drain and spread out on a tray for 20 minutes, stirring it occasionally with your fingers.

2 Meanwhile, in a large saucepan, heat the oil and fry the vegetables for about 10 minutes, stirring from time to time.

3 Add the ginger, garlic and spices, stir well and cook for 2 minutes. Pour in the lentils, tomatoes, stock and raisins, and add seasoning.

4 Bring to a boil, then turn down to a simmer. By this time the couscous should be ready for steaming. Place in a steamer and fit this on top of the stew.

5 Cover and steam gently for about 20 minutes. The grains should be swollen and soft. Fork through and season well. Spoon into a serving dish.

6 Add the lemon rind and juice to the stew and check the seasoning. If liked, add harissa paste to taste; it is quite hot so beware! Serve the stew from a casserole dish separately. Spoon the couscous onto a plate and ladle the stew on top.

Cabbage Roulades with Lemon Sauce

Cabbage or chard leaves filled with a rice and lentil stuffing and served with a light egg lemon sauce makes a light and tasty main course.

SERVES 4–6
12 large cabbage or chard leaves, stalks removed
salt
2 tbsp sunflower oil
1 onion, chopped
1 large carrot, grated
4 oz sliced mushrooms
2½ cups stock
½ cup long grain rice
4 tbsp red lentils
1 tsp dried oregano or marjoram
ground black pepper
3½ oz soft cheese with garlic
SAUCE
3 tbsp all-purpose flour
juice of 1 lemon
3 eggs, beaten

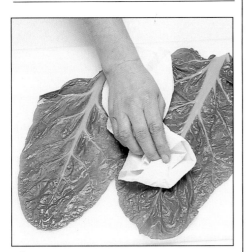

1 Blanch the leaves in boiling, salted water until they begin to wilt. Drain, reserve the water and pat the leaves dry with paper towel.

2 Heat the oil and lightly fry the onion, carrot and mushrooms for 5 minutes, and then pour in the stock.

3 Add the rice, lentils, herbs and seasoning. Bring to a boil, cover and simmer gently for 15 minutes. Remove from the heat, then stir in the cheese. Preheat the oven to 375°F.

4 Lay out the chard or cabbage leaves rib side down, and spoon on the filling at the stalk end. Fold the sides in and roll up.

5 Place the join side down in a small roasting pan and pour in the reserved cabbage water. Cover with lightly greased foil and bake for 30–45 minutes until the leaves are tender.

6 Remove the cabbage rolls from the oven, drain over a bowl and place on a serving dish. Strain 2½ cups of the cooking water into a saucepan and bring to a boil.

7 Blend the flour to a runny paste with a little cold water and whisk into the boiling stock, together with the lemon juice.

8 Beat the eggs in a heatproof bowl and slowly pour on the hot stock, whisking well as you go.

9 Return to the stove and on the lowest heat, stir until smooth and thick. Do not allow the sauce to boil or it will start to curdle. Serve the rolls with some of the sauce poured over and the rest passed round separately.

Irish Colcannon

This lovely warming winter dish bears a slight resemblance to Eggs Florentine. Here, baked eggs nestle among creamy potatoes with curly kale or cabbage and a topping of grated cheese.

SERVES 4
2 lb potatoes, cut in even pieces
8 oz curly kale or crisp green cabbage, shredded
2 scallions, chopped
butter or margarine, to taste
fresh nutmeg, grated
salt and ground black pepper
4 large eggs
3 oz aged cheese, grated

1 Boil the potatoes until just tender, then drain and mash well.

2 Lightly cook the kale or cabbage until just tender but still crisp. Preheat the oven to 375°F.

3 Drain the greens and mix them into the potato with the scallions, butter or margarine and nutmeg. Season to taste.

4 Spoon the mixture into a shallow ovenproof dish and make four hollows in the mixture. Break an egg into each and season well.

5 Bake for about 12 minutes or until the eggs are just set, then serve sprinkled with the cheese.

Pasta with Caponata

The Sicilians have an excellent sweet and sour vegetable dish called *caponata*, which naturally enough goes wonderfully well with pasta.

SERVES 4
1 medium eggplant, cut into sticks
2 medium zucchini, cut into sticks
8 baby onions, peeled or 1 large onion, sliced
2 garlic cloves, crushed
1 large red pepper, sliced
4 tbsp olive oil, preferably highly flavored extra virgin
scant 2 cups tomato juice or 1 × 17 fl oz carton puréed tomatoes
2/3 cup water
2 tbsp balsamic vinegar
juice of 1 lemon
1 tbsp sugar
2 tbsp sliced black olives
2 tbsp capers
salt and ground black pepper
14 oz tagliatelle or other long pasta ribbons

1 Lightly salt the eggplant and zucchini and leave them to drain in a colander for 30 minutes. Rinse thoroughly and pat dry with paper towel.

2 In a large saucepan, lightly fry the onions, garlic and pepper in the oil for 5 minutes, then stir in the eggplant and zucchini and fry for a further 5 minutes.

3 Stir in the tomato juice or puréed tomatoes, along with the water. Stir well, bringing the mixture to a boil, then add all the rest of the ingredients except the pasta. Season to taste and then simmer for 10 minutes.

4 Meanwhile, boil the pasta according to the instructions on the package, then drain. Serve the caponata with the pasta.

Spinach Gnocchi

This wholesome Italian dish is ideal for making in advance then baking when required. Serve it with a fresh tomato sauce.

SERVES 4–6
14 oz fresh leaf spinach, well washed, or 6 oz frozen leaf spinach, thawed
good 3 cups milk
1¼ cups semolina
4 tbsp butter, melted
2 oz Parmesan cheese, freshly grated, plus extra to serve
fresh nutmeg, grated
salt and ground black pepper
2 eggs, beaten

2 In a large saucepan, heat the milk and when just on the point of boiling, sprinkle in the semolina in a steady stream, stirring it briskly with a wooden spoon.

5 Stamp out shapes using a plain round cutter with a diameter of about 1½ in. Reserve the trimmings.

1 Blanch the spinach in the tiniest amount of water, then drain and squeeze dry through a sieve with the back of a ladle. Chop the spinach roughly.

3 Simmer the semolina for 2 minutes then remove from the heat and stir in half the butter, most of the cheese, nutmeg and seasoning to taste and the spinach. Allow to cool for 5 minutes.

6 Grease a shallow ovenproof dish. Place the trimmings on the base and arrange the gnocchi rounds on top with each one overlapping.

7 Brush the tops with the remaining butter and sprinkle over the last of the grated cheese.

8 Preheat the oven when ready to bake to 375°F and cook for about 35 minutes until golden and crisp on top. Serve hot with fresh tomato sauce and extra cheese.

VARIATION

For a special occasion, make half plain and half spinach gnocchi and arrange in an attractive pattern to serve. Use the same recipe as above but halve the amount of spinach and add to half the mixture in a separate bowl to make two batches. Stamp out and cook the gnocchi as normal. For a more substantial, healthy meal, make a tasty vegetable base of lightly sautéed peppers, zucchini and mushrooms and place the gnocchi on the top.

4 Stir in the eggs then tip the mixture out onto a shallow baking sheet, spreading it out to a ½ in. thickness. Allow to cool completely, then chill until solid.

Red Rice Rissoles

Arborio rice chills to a firm texture, yet remains light and creamy when reheated as crisp crumbed rissoles. These contain small nuggets of cheese for extra creaminess.

SERVES ABOUT 8
1 large red onion, chopped
1 red pepper, chopped
2 garlic cloves, crushed
1 red chili, finely chopped
2 tbsp olive oil
2 tbsp butter
1¼ cups Arborio rice
4½ cups stock
4 sun-dried tomatoes, chopped
2 tbsp tomato paste
2 tsp dried oregano
salt and ground black pepper
3 tbsp fresh parsley, chopped
6 oz cheese, e.g. smoked Gouda or
　aged Cheddar
1 egg, beaten
1 cup dried bread crumbs
oil, for deep frying

1 Fry the onion, pepper, garlic and chili in the oil and butter for 5 minutes. Stir in the rice and fry for a further 2 minutes.

2 Pour in the stock and add the tomatoes, paste, oregano and seasoning. Bring to a boil, stirring occasionally, then cover and simmer for 20 minutes.

3 Stir in the parsley, then turn into a shallow dish and chill until firm. When cold, divide the mixture into 12 and shape into balls.

4 Cut the cheese into 12 pieces and press a nugget into the center of each of the rissoles.

5 Put the beaten egg in one bowl and the bread crumbs into another. Dip the rissoles first into the egg then into the bread crumbs, coating each one evenly.

6 Lay the coated rissoles on a plate and chill again for 30 minutes. Fill a deep fat frying pan one-third full of oil and heat until a cube of day-old bread browns in under a minute.

7 Fry the rissoles in batches, reheating the oil in between, for about 3–4 minutes. Drain on paper towel and keep warm, uncovered, before serving.

Broad Bean and Cauliflower Curry

A tasty mid-week curry to serve with rice (especially a brown basmati), small papadums and maybe a cool cucumber raita.

SERVES 4
2 garlic cloves, chopped
1 in cube fresh ginger root
1 fresh green chili, seeded and chopped
1 tbsp oil
1 onion, sliced
1 large potato, chopped
2 tbsp ghee or softened butter
1 tbsp curry powder, mild or hot
1 medium size cauliflower, cut into small
  florets
2½ cups stock
2 tbsp creamed coconut
salt and ground black pepper
1 × 10 oz can broad beans, with liquor
juice of half a lemon (optional)
fresh coriander or parsley, chopped,
  to serve

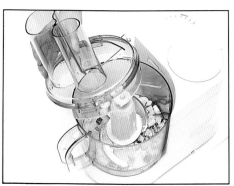

1 Blend the garlic, ginger, chili and oil in a food processor until they form a smooth paste.

2 In a large saucepan, fry the onion and potato in the ghee or butter for 5 minutes then stir in the spice paste and curry powder. Cook for 1 minute.

3 Add the cauliflower florets and stir well into the spicy mixture, then pour in the stock. Bring to a boil and mix in the coconut, stirring until it melts.

4 Season well, then cover and simmer for 10 minutes. Add the beans and their liquor and cook uncovered for a further 10 minutes.

5 Check the seasoning and add a good squeeze of lemon juice if liked. Serve hot garnished with coriander or parsley.

SALADS
&
VEGETABLE DISHES

Here is a delightful range of colorful salads and delicious
vegetable dishes and accompaniments. Varied but easy to obtain
ingredients ensure the perfect recipe for every style of meal.

Bean Sprout Stir-fry

Home grown bean sprouts taste so good, tossed into a tasty stir-fry. They have more flavor and texture than store-bought varieties and are very nutritious, being rich in vitamins and high in fiber. (Old dried beans will not sprout, so use beans that are well within their "Use by" date).

SERVES 3–4
2 tbsp sunflower or groundnut oil
8 oz mixed sprouted beans
2 scallions, chopped
1 garlic clove, crushed
2 tbsp soy sauce
2 tsp sesame oil
1 tbsp sesame seeds
2 tbsp fresh coriander or parsley, chopped
salt and ground black pepper

1 Heat the sunflower or groundnut oil in a large wok and stir-fry the sprouting beans, scallions and garlic for 5 minutes.

2 Add the remaining ingredients, cook for 1–2 minutes more and serve hot.

HOME SPROUTING BEANS

Use any of the following pulses to grow your own sprouting beans: green or brown lentils, aduki beans, mung beans, chick peas, navy and white beans, soy beans or Indian massor dal.

Cover 3 tbsp of your chosen pulses with lukewarm water. Leave to soak overnight, then drain and rinse thoroughly.

Place in a large clean jam jar or special sprouting tray. Cover with muslin and secure with a rubber band. If using a jam jar, lay the jar on its side and shake it so the beans spread along the length. Leave somewhere warm.

Rinse the beans night and morning with plenty of cold water, running this through the muslin, and drain. Carefully place the jar back on its side.

Repeat this twice a day until roots and shoots appear. (If nothing happens after 48 hours, the beans are probably too old). When the shoots are at least twice the length of the bean, rinse for the last time and store in the fridge for up to two days.

Panzanella Salad

If sliced juicy tomatoes layered with day old bread sounds strange for a salad, don't be deceived – it's quite delicious. A popular Italian salad, this dish is ideal as a starter or an accompaniment. Use full-flavored tomatoes for the best result.

SERVES 4–6
4 thick slices day-old bread, either white, brown or rye
1 small red onion, thinly sliced
1 lb ripe tomatoes, thinly sliced
4 oz Mozzarella cheese, thinly sliced
1 tbsp fresh basil, shredded, or marjoram
salt and ground black pepper
½ cup extra virgin olive oil
3 tbsp balsamic vinegar
juice of 1 small lemon
pitted and sliced black olives or salted capers, to garnish

1 Dip the bread briefly in cold water, then carefully squeeze out the excess water. Arrange on the bottom of a shallow salad bowl.

2 Soak the onion slices in cold water for about 10 minutes while you prepare the other ingredients. Drain and reserve.

3 Layer the tomatoes, cheese, onion and basil or marjoram, seasoning well in between each layer. Sprinkle with oil, vinegar and lemon juice.

4 Top with the olives or capers, cover with plastic wrap and then chill in the refrigerator overnight, if possible.

Caesar's Salad

On Independence Day 1924, in Tijuana, Mexico, a restauranteur – Caesar Cardini – created this masterpiece of new American cuisine. It has all the elements of a good salad – being light, flavorsome, attractive and nutritious with a good crunch.

SERVES 4
2 thick slices crustless bread
2 garlic cloves
sunflower oil, for frying
1 Romaine lettuce, washed and torn in pieces
½ cup fresh Parmesan cheese, coarsely grated
2 eggs
DRESSING
2 tbsp extra virgin olive oil
2 tsp French mustard
2 tsp Worcestershire sauce
2 tbsp fresh lemon juice

1 Cut the bread into cubes. Heat one of the garlic cloves slowly in about 3 tbsp of the sunflower oil in a saucepan and then toss in the bread cubes. Remove the garlic clove.

2 Heat the oven to 375°F. Spread the garlicky cubes on a baking sheet and bake the bread for about 10–12 minutes until golden and crisp. Remove and allow to cool completely.

3 Rub the inside of a large salad bowl with the remaining garlic clove and then discard it.

4 Toss in the torn lettuce, sprinkling between the leaves with the cheese. Cover and set the salad aside.

5 Boil a small saucepan of water and cook the eggs for 1 minute only. Remove the eggs, and crack them open into a jug or bowl. The whites should be milky and the yolks raw.

6 Whisk the dressing ingredients into the eggs. When ready to serve pour the dressing over the leaves, toss well together and serve topped with the croûtons.

VARIATION

Why not try a refreshing Italian version of this salad? Use cubed ciabatta bread for the croûtons. Rub the inside of a salad bowl with garlic and spoon in 2–3 tbsp of good olive oil. Add a selection of torn salad leaves, including arugula, together with some shaved Parmesan cheese. Do not mix yet. Just before serving, add the croûtons, season well, then toss the leaves with the oil, coating well. Finally, squeeze over the juice of a fresh lemon.

Chef's Salad

This is basically whatever you make of it – a lovely large salad containing all your favorite ingredients. It is also a good opportunity to use up leftover vegetables and small pieces of cheese from the refrigerator. For these reasons, quantities are approximate.

SERVES 6
1 lb new potatoes, halved if large
2 carrots, coarsely grated
½ small fennel bulb or 2 stalks celery, sliced thinly
2 oz sliced button mushrooms
¼ cucumber, sliced or chopped
small green or red pepper, sliced
4 tbsp peas
1 cup cooked pulses, e.g. red kidney beans or green lentils
1 Boston or red leaf lettuce, or 1 head chicory
2–3 hard-boiled eggs, quartered, and/or grated cheese, to serve
small bunch watercress, snipped

1 Put all the vegetables and pulses (except the lettuce or chicory) into a large mixing bowl.

DRESSING
4 tbsp mayonnaise
3 tbsp natural yogurt
2 tbsp milk
2 tbsp chopped fresh chives or scallion tops
salt and ground black pepper

2 Line a large platter with the lettuce or chicory leaves – creating a nest for the other salad ingredients. Mix the dressing ingredients together and pour over the salad in the mixing bowl.

3 Toss the salad thoroughly in the dressing, season well then pile into the center of the lettuce or chicory nest.

4 Top the salad with the eggs, cheese or both and sprinkle with the snipped watercress. Serve lightly chilled.

Potato and Radish Salad 🌿

So many potato salads are dressed in thick sauce. This one is quite light and colorful with a flavorsome yet delicate dressing.

SERVES 4–6
1 lb new potatoes, scrubbed
3 tbsp olive oil
1 tbsp walnut or hazelnut oil (optional)
2 tbsp wine vinegar
2 tsp coarse grain mustard
1 tsp honey
salt and ground black pepper
about 6–8 radishes, thinly sliced
2 tbsp fresh chives, chopped

1 Boil the potatoes until just tender. Drain, return to the pan and cut any large potatoes in half.

2 Make a dressing with the oils, vinegar, mustard, honey and seasoning. Mix them together thoroughly in a bowl.

3 Toss the dressing into the potatoes while they are still cooling and allow them to stand for an hour or so.

4 Mix in the radishes and chives, chill lightly, toss again and serve.

COOK'S TIP

The secret of a good potato salad is to dress the potatoes while still warm in a vinaigrette-style dressing in order to let them soak up the flavor as they cool. You can then mix in an additional creamy dressing of mayonnaise and natural yogurt if liked. Sliced celery, red onion and chopped walnuts would make a good alternative to the radishes and, for best effect, serve on a platter lined with frilly lettuce leaves.

Thai Rice and Sprouting Beans

Thai rice has a delicate fragrance and texture that is delicious whether served hot or cold. This salad is a colorful collection of popular Thai flavors and textures.

SERVES 6
2 tbsp sesame oil
2 tbsp fresh lime juice
1 small fresh red chili, seeded and chopped
1 garlic clove, crushed
2 tsp fresh ginger root, grated
2 tbsp light soy sauce
1 tsp honey
3 tbsp pineapple juice
1 tbsp wine vinegar
1¼ cups Thai fragrant rice, boiled
2 scallions, sliced
2 rings canned pineapple in natural juice, chopped
1¼ cups sprouted lentils or bean sprouts
1 small red pepper, sliced
1 stalk celery, sliced
½ cup unsalted cashew nuts, roughly chopped
2 tbsp toasted sesame seeds
salt and ground black pepper

1 Whisk together the sesame oil, lime juice, chili, garlic, ginger, soy sauce, honey, pineapple juice and vinegar in a large bowl. Stir in the lightly boiled rice.

2 Toss in all the remaining ingredients and mix well. This dish can be served warm or lightly chilled. If the rice grains stick together on cooling, simply stir them with a metal spoon.

Chicory, Carrot and Arugula Salad

A bright and colorful salad which is ideal for a buffet or barbecue party. Use watercress if you are unable to obtain any arugula.

SERVES 4–6
3 carrots, coarsely grated
about 2 oz fresh arugula or watercress, roughly chopped
1 large head chicory
DRESSING:
3 tbsp sunflower oil
1 tbsp hazelnut or walnut oil (optional)
2 tbsp cider or wine vinegar
2 tsp honey
1 tsp grated lemon rind
1 tbsp poppy seeds
salt and ground black pepper

1 Mix the carrot and arugula or watercress together in a large bowl and season well.

2 Shake the dressing ingredients together in a screw top jar then pour onto the carrot and greenery. Toss the salad thoroughly.

3 Line a shallow salad bowl with the chicory leaves and spoon the salad into the center. Serve lightly chilled.

Bountiful Bean and Nut Salad 🥬

This is a good multi-purpose dish. It can be a cold main course, a buffet party dish, or a salad on the side. It also keeps well for up to three days in the refrigerator.

SERVES 6

½ cup red kidney, pinto or borlotti beans
½ cup white cannellini or lima beans
2 tbsp olive oil
6 oz cut fresh green beans
3 scallions, sliced
1 small yellow or red pepper, sliced
1 carrot, coarsely grated
2 tbsp dried onion flakes or sun-dried tomatoes, chopped
½ cup unsalted cashew nuts or almonds, split in half

DRESSING

3 tbsp sunflower oil
2 tbsp red wine vinegar
1 tbsp coarse grain mustard
1 tsp superfine sugar
1 tsp dried mixed herbs
salt and ground black pepper

1 Soak the beans, overnight if possible, then drain and rinse well, cover with a lot of cold water and cook according to the instructions on the package.

2 When cooked, drain and season the beans and toss them in the olive oil. Leave to cool for 30 minutes.

3 In a large bowl, mix in the other vegetables, including the sun-dried tomatoes but not the dried onion flakes, if using, or the nuts.

4 Make up the dressing by shaking all the ingredients together in a screw top jar. Toss the dressing into the salad and check the seasoning again. Serve sprinkled with the onion flakes, if using, and the split nuts.

Garden Salad and Garlic Crostini 🥬

Dress a colorful mixture of salad
leaves with good olive oil and freshly
squeezed lemon juice, then top it with
crispy bread crostini.

SERVES 4–6
3 thick slices day old bread, e.g. ciabatta
½ cup extra virgin olive oil
garlic clove, cut
½ small Boston or Romaine lettuce
½ small oak leaf lettuce
1 oz arugula leaves or watercress
1 oz fresh flat leaf parsley
a few leaves and flowers of nasturtium
a small handful of young dandelion
  leaves
sea salt flakes and ground black pepper
juice of 1 fresh lemon

1 Cut the bread into medium size dice
about ½ in square.

2 Heat half the oil gently in a frying pan
and fry the bread cubes in it, tossing them
until they are well coated and lightly
browned. Remove and cool.

3 Rub the inside of a large salad bowl
with the garlic and discard. Pour the rest
of the oil into the bottom of the bowl.

4 Wash, dry and tear the leaves into bite
size pieces and pile them into the bowl.
Season with salt and pepper. Cover and
keep chilled until ready to serve.

5 To serve, toss the leaves in the oil at
the bottom of the bowl, then sprinkle with
the lemon juice and toss again. Scatter
over the crostini and serve immediately.

Californian Salad

Full of vitality and vitamins, this is a lovely light healthy salad for sunny days when you need an extra boost.

SERVES 4
1 small crisp lettuce, torn in pieces
8 oz young spinach leaves, well washed
2 carrots, coarsely grated
4 oz cherry tomatoes, halved
2 celery stalks, thinly sliced
½ cup raisins
½ cup blanched almonds or unsalted cashew nuts, halved
2 tbsp sunflower seeds
2 tbsp sesame seeds, lightly toasted
DRESSING:
3 tbsp extra virgin olive oil
2 tbsp cider vinegar
2 tsp honey
juice of 1 small orange
salt and ground black pepper

1 Put the salad vegetables, raisins, almonds or cashew nuts and seeds into a large bowl.

2 Put all the dressing ingredients into a screw top jar, shake them up well and pour over the salad.

3 Toss the salad thoroughly and divide it between four small salad bowls. Season and serve lightly chilled.

Scandinavian Cucumber and Dill

It's amazing what a light touch of salt can do to simple cucumber slices. They take on a contradictory soft yet crisp texture and develop a good, full flavor. However, juices continue to form after salting, so this salad is best dressed just before serving. It is particularly complementary to hot and spicy food.

SERVES 4
2 cucumbers
salt
2 tbsp fresh chives, chopped
2 tbsp fresh dill, chopped
⅔ cup sour cream or natural yogurt
ground black pepper

1 Slice the cucumbers as thinly as possible, preferably in a food processor or a slicer.

2 Place the slices in layers in a colander set over a plate to catch the juices. Sprinkling each layer well, but not too heavily, with salt.

3 Leave the cucumber to drain for up to 2 hours, then lay out the slices on a clean dish towel and pat them dry.

4 Mix the cucumber with the herbs, cream or yogurt and plenty of pepper. Serve as soon as possible.

COOK'S TIP

Deseeded and lightly salted cucumbers are also delicious as sandwich fillings in wafer thin buttered brown bread. These sandwiches were always served at traditional tea parties.

Useful Dressings

A good dressing can make even the simplest combination of fresh vegetables a memorable treat. Remember, in addition to normal salads, lightly cooked hot vegetables such as carrots and potatoes or pulses and grains absorb more flavor and are less greasy if dressed while hot.

Home made Mayonnaise
Make this by hand, if possible. If you make it in a food processor, it will be noticeably lighter.

2 egg yolks
½ tsp salt
½ tsp dry mustard
ground black pepper
1¼ cups sunflower oil, or half olive and half sunflower oil
1 tbsp wine vinegar
1 tbsp hot water

1 Put the yolks into a bowl with the salt and mustard and a grinding of pepper.

2 Stand the bowl on a damp dish cloth. Using a whisk, beat the yolks and the seasoning thoroughly, then beat in a small trickle of oil.

3 Continue trickling in the oil, adding it in very small amounts. The secret of a good, thick mayonnaise is to add the oil very slowly, beating each addition well before you add more. When all the oil is added, mix in the vinegar and hot water.

To make mayonnaise in a blender, use one whole egg and one yolk instead of two yolks. Blend the eggs with the seasonings. Then, with the blades running, trickle in the oil very slowly. Add the vinegar.

Original Thousand Islands Dressing

4 tbsp sunflower oil
1 tbsp fresh orange juice
1 tbsp fresh lemon juice
2 tsp grated lemon rind
1 tbsp finely chopped onion
1 tsp paprika
1 tsp Worcestershire sauce
1 tbsp finely chopped parsley
salt and ground black pepper

Put all the ingredients into a screw top jar, season to taste and shake vigorously. Great with green salads, grated carrot and hot potato, pasta and rice salads.

Yogurt Dressing

⅔ cup natural yogurt
2 tbsp mayonnaise
2 tbsp milk
1 tbsp fresh parsley, chopped
1 tbsp fresh chives or scallions, chopped
salt and ground black pepper

Simply mix all the ingredients together thoroughly in a bowl.

Peperonata with Raisins

Sliced roasted peppers in dressing with vinegar-soaked raisins make a tasty side salad which complements many other dishes and is quick to make, especially if you already have a batch of peppers in oil.

SERVES 2–4
6 tbsp sliced red or green peppers in olive oil, drained
1 tbsp onion, chopped
2 tbsp balsamic vinegar
3 tbsp raisins
2 tbsp fresh parsley, chopped
ground black pepper

1 Toss the peppers with the onion and leave to steep for an hour.

2 Put the vinegar and raisins in a small saucepan and heat for a minute, then allow to cool.

3 Mix all the ingredients together thoroughly and spoon into a serving bowl. Serve lightly chilled.

VARIATION

Peperonata is one of the classic Italian antipasto dishes, served at the start of each meal with crusty bread to mop up the delicious juices. Try serving shavings of fresh Parmesan cheese alongside, or buy a good selection of green and black olives to accompany the peperonata. Small baby tomatoes will complete the antipasto.

Spinach Roulade

A simple purée of spinach baked with eggs rolled around a creamy red pepper filling makes an exotic and colorful side dish. Even better, this can be prepared in advance and then reheated when required.

SERVES 4

1 lb leaf spinach, well washed and
    drained
fresh nutmeg, grated
2 tbsp butter, softened
3 tbsp Parmesan cheese, grated
3 tbsp heavy cream
salt and ground black pepper
2 eggs, separated
1 small red pepper, chopped
7 oz soft cheese with garlic and herbs

---

1 Line a medium size jelly roll pan with waxed paper and grease the paper. Preheat the oven to 375°F.

2 Cook the spinach with a tiny amount of water then drain well, pressing it through a sieve with the back of a ladle. Chop the spinach finely.

3 Mix the spinach with the nutmeg, butter, Parmesan cheese, cream and seasoning. Cool for 5 minutes, then beat in the egg yolks.

4 Whisk the egg whites until they form soft peaks and carefully fold in to the spinach mixture. Spread in to the prepared pan, level and bake for 12–15 minutes until firm.

5 Turn the spinach out upside down on to a clean dish towel and allow it to cool in the pan for half an hour.

6 Meanwhile, simmer the pepper in about 2 tbsp of water in a covered pan until just soft, then either purée it in a blender or chop it finely. Mix with the soft cheese and season well.

7 When the spinach has cooled, peel off the paper. Trim any hard edges and spread it with the red pepper cream.

8 Carefully roll up the spinach and pepper in the dish towel, leave for 10 minutes to firm up, then serve on a long platter, cut in thick slices.

VARIATION

A thick vegetable purée of any root vegetable also works well as a roulade. Try cooked beets or parsnip, flavoring lightly with a mild curry-style spice such as cumin or coriander. The fillings can be varied too, such as finely chopped and sautéed mushroom and onion, or grated carrot mixed with yogurt and chives. Roulades are delicious served warm as well. Sprinkle with cheese and bake in a moderately hot oven for 15 minutes or so.

Mighty Mushrooms

There is now a wide variety of cultivated mushrooms on sale in larger supermarkets and greengrocers so a simple side dish of mushrooms becomes quite exciting. This also makes an excellent sauce to serve tossed into pasta. Dried ceps or porcini mushrooms are on sale in delicatessens if you have trouble finding them in supermarkets.

SERVES 4
½ oz package dried porcini mushrooms/
 ceps (optional)
4 tbsp olive oil
8 oz button mushrooms, halved or sliced
4 oz oyster mushrooms
4 oz fresh shiitake mushrooms, or 1 oz
 dried and soaked mushrooms
2 garlic cloves, crushed
2 tsp ground coriander
salt and ground black pepper
3 tbsp fresh parsley, chopped

1 If you are using porcini mushrooms (and they do give a good rich flavor), soak them in a little hot water just to cover for 20 minutes.

2 In a large saucepan, heat the oil and add all the mushrooms, including the soaked porcinis, if using. Stir well, cover and cook gently for 5 minutes.

3 Stir in the garlic, coriander and seasoning. Cook for another 5 minutes until the mushrooms are tender and much of the liquor has been reduced.

4 Mix in the parsley, allow to cool slightly and serve.

Tomato Sauce

A basic sauce which can either be part of a larger recipe or served as a side sauce. For extra flavor, add red pepper, or vary the taste with orange rind and juice, chopped fresh herbs such as basil, or spice it up with some chili sauce.

SERVES 4–6
1 onion, chopped
2 garlic cloves, crushed
1 small red pepper (optional), chopped
3 tbsp olive oil
1½ lb fresh tomatoes, skinned and
 chopped, or 1 × 14 oz can chopped
 tomatoes
1 tsp granulated sugar
salt and ground black pepper
2 tbsp fresh herbs, chopped, e.g. basil,
 parsley, marjoram (optional)

1 Gently fry the onion, garlic and red pepper, if using, in the oil for 5 minutes until they are soft.

2 Stir in the tomatoes, add the sugar and seasoning to taste, bring to a boil then cover and simmer for 15–20 minutes.

3 The sauce should now be thick and pulpy. If it is a little thin, then boil it – uncovered – so that it reduces down. Stir in the fresh herbs, if using, and then check the seasoning.

COOK'S TIP

Why not make up a large batch of this sauce and freeze it in two-portion sizes?

Indian Spiced Okra with Almonds

Long and elegantly shaped, it is not surprising these vegetables have the popular name of "lady's fingers." Although commonly used in many international dishes, okra are particularly well suited to all the Indian spices.

SERVES 2–4
8 oz okra
½ cup blanched almonds, chopped
2 tbsp butter
1 tbsp sunflower oil
2 garlic cloves, crushed
1 in cube fresh ginger root, grated
1 tsp cumin seeds
1 tsp ground coriander
1 tsp paprika

1 Trim just the tops of the okra stems and around the edges of the stalks. They have a sticky liquid which oozes out if prepared too far ahead, so trim them immediately before cooking.

2 In a shallow fireproof dish, fry the almonds in the butter until they are lightly golden, then remove.

3 Add the oil to the pan and fry the okra, stirring constantly, for 2 minutes.

4 Add the garlic and ginger and fry gently for a minute, then add the spices and cook for another minute or so, stirring all the time.

VARIATION

Okra are also popular in Louisiana cooking and are an essential ingredient for gumbo, a thick, spicy stew served over hot, steaming rice. Indeed, 'gumbo' was the old African word for okra used by the American slaves. You can make a ratatouille-style vegetable stew using okra instead of eggplant, and adding onions, peppers, garlic and tomatoes. Or try them sliced, fried in garlic and spices, then stirred into a pilaf of basmati rice with cauliflower florets and carrots. This makes a colorful and delicious dish – especially when topped with crushed grilled papadums.

5 Pour in approximately 1¼ cups of water. Season well, cover and simmer for about 5 minutes or so until the okra feel just tender.

6 Finally, mix in the fried almonds and serve piping hot.

Stir-fried Cabbage

An often under-rated vegetable, crisp cabbage is wonderful when lightly cooked the Chinese way in a wok. Any cabbage will do, but perhaps the Savoy cabbage is the nicest.

SERVES 4
½ small cabbage
2 tbsp sunflower oil
1 tbsp light soy sauce
1 tbsp fresh lemon juice (optional)
2 tsp caraway seeds
ground black pepper

1 Cut the central core from the cabbage, and shred the leaves finely.

2 Heat the oil until quite hot in a wok and then stir-fry the cabbage for about 2 minutes.

3 Toss in the soy sauce, lemon juice, if using, caraway seeds and pepper, to taste.

Perfect Creamed Potatoes

If a bowl of plain, mashed potatoes sounds boring, then try serving it this way – in the French style.

SERVES 4
2 lb potatoes, peeled and diced
3 tbsp extra virgin olive oil
about ⅔ cup hot milk
fresh nutmeg, grated
salt and ground black pepper
a few leaves fresh basil or sprigs fresh
  parsley, chopped

COOK'S TIP

Choosing the right potato makes all the difference to creamed or mashed potatoes. A waxy variety won't be light and fluffy, and a potato which breaks down too quickly on boiling will become a slurry when mashed. Most bags of potatoes carry guidelines on what method of cooking they are suited for. In general, red potatoes will make a good mash, as will Florida Creamers and Yukon Golds.

1 Boil the potatoes until just tender and not too mushy. Drain very well. Ideally press the potatoes through a special potato "ricer" (rather like a large garlic press) or mash them well with a potato masher. Do not pass them through a food processor or you will have a gluey mess.

2 Beat the olive oil into the potato and mix in just enough hot milk to make a smooth, thick purée.

3 Flavor to taste with the nutmeg and seasoning, then stir in the fresh chopped herbs. Spoon into a warm serving dish and serve as soon as possible.

Roasted Peppers in Oil

Peppers take on a delicious, smoky flavor if roasted in a very hot oven. The skins can easily be peeled off and the flesh stored in olive oil. This oil can then be used to add extra flavor to salad dressings.

6 large peppers of differing colors
scant 2 cups olive oil

1 Preheat the oven to the highest temperature, about 450°F. Lightly grease a large baking sheet.

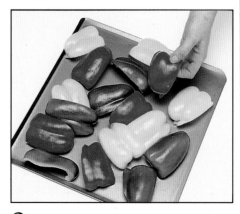

2 Quarter the peppers, remove the cores and seeds then squash them flat with the back of your hands. Lay the peppers skin side up on the baking tray.

3 Roast the peppers at the top of the oven until the skins blacken and blister. This will take about 12–15 minutes.

4 Remove the peppers from the oven, cover with a clean dish towel until they are cool, then peel off the skins.

5 Slice the peppers and pack them into a clean preserving jar.

6 Add the oil to the jar to cover the peppers completely, then seal the lid.

7 Store the peppers in the refrigerator and use them within 2 weeks. Use the oil in dressings or for cooking once the peppers have been eaten.

COOK'S TIP

These pepper slices make very attractive presents, especially around Christmas time. You can either buy special preserving jars from kitchen equipment shops, or wash out large jam jars, soaking off the labels at the same time. The jars should then be sterilized by placing upside down in a low oven for about half an hour. Fill the jars while still hot with the sliced peppers, and fill with a good olive oil. Cover immediately with the lid and fix on an attractive label.

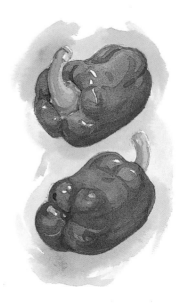

Ove ... asties 🌿

Very po ... a
much b ... he
family t ... s.

SERVES ...
4 medium to large baking potatoes
⅔ cup olive oil
1 tsp dried mixed herbs (optional)
sea salt flakes

1 Preheat the oven to the highest possible temperature, generally 450°F. Place a lightly oiled roasting pan in the oven to get really hot.

2 Cut the potatoes in half lengthwise, then into long thin wedges. Brush each side lightly with oil.

3 When the oven is really hot, remove the pan carefully and scatter the potato slices over it in a single layer.

4 Sprinkle the potatoes with the herbs and salt and place in the oven for about 20 minutes or until they are golden brown, crisp and lightly puffy. Serve immediately.

VARIATION

Parsnips also make fine oven chips. Choose large parsnips which tend to have more flavor. Slice thinly on a diagonal and roast in the same way as above, although you may find they do not take as long to cook. They make great mid-week suppers for kids and grown-ups served with fried eggs, mushrooms and tomatoes.

Warm Spicy Dhal

If you thought split yellow peas were only for soups, then try this Indian inspired dish. Serve with rice, chappatis or naan bread and whatever main dish you like – perhaps eggs, fried eggplant, or even a tasty dish of fried mushrooms.

SERVES 4–6
8 oz yellow split peas
2 onions, chopped
1 large bay leaf
2½ cups stock or water
salt and ground black pepper
2 tsp black mustard seeds
2 tbsp butter, melted
1 garlic clove, crushed
1 in cube fresh ginger root, grated
1 small green pepper, sliced
1 tsp ground turmeric
1 tsp garam masala or mild curry powder
3 tomatoes, skinned and chopped
fresh coriander or parsley, to serve

1 Put the split peas, 1 onion and the bay leaf in the stock or water, in a covered pan. Simmer for 25 minutes, seasoning lightly towards the end.

2 In a separate pan, fry the mustard seeds in the butter for about 30 seconds until they start to pop, then add all the remaining onion, along with the garlic, ginger and green pepper.

3 Sauté for about 5 minutes until softened, then stir in the remaining spices and fry for a few seconds more.

4 Add the split peas, tomatoes, and a little extra water if it needs it. Cover and simmer for a further 10 minutes, then check the seasoning and serve hot garnished with coriander or parsley.

Potato Latkes

These little potato pancakes make a pleasant and unusual alternative to chips or roast potatoes.

MAKES ABOUT 24
2 lb potatoes, peeled and coarsely grated
scant ½ cup self-rising flour
2 eggs
1 tbsp onion, grated
fresh nutmeg, grated
salt and ground black pepper
oil, for shallow frying

1 Soak the grated potato in plenty of cold water for about an hour, then drain well and pat dry with a clean dish towel.

2 Beat together the flour, eggs, onion and nutmeg, then mix in the potato. Season well.

3 Heat a thin layer of oil in a heavy based frying pan and drop about a tablespoon of potato batter into the pan, squashing it flat, if necessary.

4 Cook the potato until golden brown, then flip over and cook the other side. Drain on paper towel and keep warm, uncovered, in the oven. Repeat with the rest of the mixture.

Stir-fried Eggplant

A speedy side dish with an Oriental touch. The eggplant is stir-fried with red pepper and black beans which give it a really exotic and colorful appearance. Salted black beans are sold either dried or canned. Dried ones will need soaking.

SERVES 4
2 tbsp groundnut oil
1 eggplant, sliced
2 scallions, sliced diagonally
1 garlic clove, crushed
1 small red pepper, sliced
2 tbsp oyster sauce
1 tbsp Chinese salted black beans, soaked if dried
ground black pepper
1 tbsp fresh coriander or parsley, chopped, to garnish

1 Heat the oil in a wok and stir-fry the eggplant for 2 minutes. Add the scallions, garlic and pepper and cook for a further 2 minutes.

2 Add the oyster sauce, black beans and pepper. Cook for a further minute, season with pepper only and serve with fresh coriander or parsley.

Peas and Lettuce

Do not discard the tough, outer leaves of lettuce – they are delicious if shredded and cooked with peas.

SERVES 4
6 outer leaves of lettuce, e.g. Boston, Cobb
1 small onion or shallot, sliced
2 tbsp butter or sunflower margarine
8 oz fresh or frozen peas
fresh nutmeg, grated
salt and ground black pepper

1 Pull off the outer lettuce leaves and wash them well. Roughly shred the leaves with your hands.

2 In a saucepan, lightly fry the lettuce and onion or shallot in the butter or margarine for 3 minutes.

3 Add the peas, nutmeg to taste and seasoning. Stir, cover and simmer for about 5 minutes. This dish can be drained or served slightly wet.

Hash Browns

A traditional American breakfast dish, hash browns can be served any time of day. They are a tasty way of using up any leftover boiled potatoes.

SERVES 4
4 tbsp sunflower or olive oil
1 lb cooked potatoes, diced
1 small onion, chopped
salt and ground black pepper

1 Heat the oil in a large, heavy-based frying pan and when quite hot add the potatoes in a single layer. Scatter the onion on top and season well.

2 Cook on a moderate heat until browned underneath, pressing down on the potatoes with a spoon or spatula to squash them together.

3 When the potatoes are nicely browned, turn them over in sections with a spatula and fry on the other side, pressing them down once again. Serve when heated through and lightly crispy.

Potato and Parsnip Dauphinoise

Layers of potatoes and parsnips are baked slowly in creamy milk with grated cheese. This is an ideal special side dish or light supper dish.

SERVES 4–6
2 lb potatoes, thinly sliced
1 onion, thinly sliced
1 lb parsnips, thinly sliced
2 garlic cloves, crushed
4 tbsp butter
4 oz Gruyère or Cheddar cheese, grated
fresh nutmeg, grated
salt and ground black pepper
1¼ cups light cream
1¼ cups milk

1 Lightly grease a large shallow ovenproof dish, and then preheat the oven to 350°F.

2 Layer the potatoes with the onion and parsnips. In between each layer, dot the vegetables with garlic and butter, sprinkle over most of the cheese, add the nutmeg and season well.

3 Heat the cream and milk together in a saucepan until they are hot but not boiling. Slowly pour the creamy milk over the vegetables, making sure it seeps underneath them.

4 Scatter the remaining cheese over the vegetables and grate a little more nutmeg on top. Bake for about an hour or so until the potatoes are tender and the cheese top is bubbling and golden.

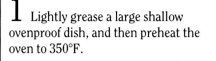

Asparagus Mimosa

Pretty spears of fresh, tender asparagus are tossed in a buttery sauce and served with a chopped egg and chervil dressing. This also makes an excellent starter.

SERVES 2
8 oz fresh asparagus
salt
ground black pepper
4 tbsp butter, melted
squeeze of fresh lemon juice
2 eggs, hard-boiled and chopped
1 tbsp fresh chervil, chopped

1 Trim the asparagus stalks and peel off the tough outer layers at the base with a vegetable peeler.

2 Poach the asparagus spears in lightly salted water, until just tender. This will take between 3–6 minutes. (Use a clean, deep frying pan if you don't have an asparagus steamer.)

3 Drain the asparagus well and arrange it on two small plates or one large one. Season well.

4 Mix the melted butter with the lemon juice. Trickle over the spears, sprinkle with the eggs and garnish with the chervil. Serve warm.

Brussels Sprouts Stir-fry

Brussels sprouts are delicious when quickly stir-fried – they are really full-flavored and their texture is full of crisp bite. Small Brussels sprouts have the best flavor.

SERVES 6
2 tbsp groundnut or sunflower oil
1 lb small Brussels sprouts, trimmed and
  halved
3 scallions, sliced
2 garlic cloves, crushed
1 small yellow pepper, sliced
2 tbsp light soy sauce
1 tbsp sesame seed oil
good pinch of granulated sugar
ground black pepper
2 tbsp sesame seeds, toasted

1 Heat the oil in a wok until quite hot, then stir-fry the sprouts for 2 minutes.

2 Add the scallions, garlic and yellow pepper and fry for another 2 minutes, stirring all the time.

3 Toss in the soy sauce, sesame seed oil, sugar, and season with pepper. Scatter over the sesame seeds and then serve immediately.

Hassleback Potatoes 🍃

These rather splendid roast potatoes are ideal to serve for dinner parties or special occasions such as Christmas. Use a good quality baking potato for the best results.

SERVES 4
olive or sunflower oil, for roasting
4 medium potatoes, peeled and halved lengthwise
salt and ground black pepper
1 tbsp plain white or whole wheat dried bread crumbs

1 Pour enough oil into a small roasting pan just to cover the base then put into an oven set at 400°F to heat.

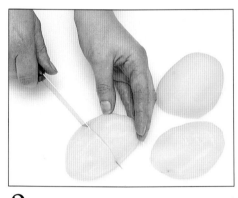

2 Meanwhile, par boil the potato halves for 5 minutes then drain. Cool slightly and slash about four times from the rounded tops almost down to the flat bottoms.

3 Place the potatoes in the heated roasting pan and spoon over the hot oil. Season well and return the potatoes to the oven for about 20 minutes.

4 Remove the potatoes once more from the oven, prise open the slashes slightly and baste with the hot oil. Sprinkle the potato tops lightly with bread crumbs and return to the oven for another 15 minutes or so until they are golden brown, cooked and crispy.

COOK'S TIP

There are many different ways of roasting potatoes in the oven. First, the choice of potato is important. Choose a variety which holds its shape well and yet is still slightly floury inside. Details on the package or bag should give you guidance. The oil is important too – choose one which is either flavorless such as sunflower or groundnut oil or one with a lot of good flavor, such as olive oil. Just before serving, try trickling a little sesame seed, walnut or hazelnut oil over the roasted potatoes for a delicious nutty flavor.

Braised Fennel and Tomato

Fennel is a very undervalued vegetable but it is excellent cooked in a light tomato sauce. This dish can be gently simmered on the stove or baked in a moderate oven.

SERVES 4–6
2 fennel bulbs
1 small onion or 3 shallots, sliced
1 garlic clove, crushed
2 tbsp olive oil
4 medium sized tomatoes, peeled and chopped
3 tbsp dry white wine
1 tbsp fresh marjoram, chopped
⅔ cup stock or water
salt and ground black pepper

1 Trim the fennel and then cut it into wedges. Reserve any fronds for a garnish.

2 Lightly sauté the fennel with the onion or shallots and garlic in the oil in a fireproof dish for 5 minutes.

3 Add the tomatoes, wine, marjoram and stock or water. Season.

4 Cover and either simmer very gently for 20 minutes, or bake in a preheated oven for 30 minutes at 375°F. Garnish with any reserved fronds of fennel and serve immediately.

Creamed Winter Vegetables

A mixture of chunky mashed root vegetables, such as carrots, parsnips and rutabaga, makes a wonderfully warming winter side dish.

SERVES 4–6
8 oz carrots, chopped
8 oz parsnips, chopped
1 small rutabaga, chopped
2 tbsp butter
2 tsp mild curry paste
salt and ground black pepper
½ cup ricotta cheese
1 tbsp fresh chives, chopped

1 Boil the carrots, parsnips and rutabaga in plenty of lightly salted water until tender. Drain the vegetables, then return them to the pan with the butter, curry paste and seasoning.

2 Mash the vegetables lightly with a fork so that you end up with a chunky purée; you want to retain a good texture.

3 Stir in the ricotta cheese and chives. Check the seasoning and serve hot. This is a good dish to prepare in advance and reheat when required.

COOK'S TIP

Vegetable purées are a popular accompaniment with any dish which could be a little on the dry side, providing a good contrast of textures and colors. Suitable vegetables are Brussels sprouts, carrots, peas, broccoli and leeks.

PARTIES
&
PICNICS

From informal meals, ideal for outdoor entertaining, to elegant and delicious dishes that will add style to special occasions, here are recipes to suit every festivity.

Spicy Potato Strudel

Wrap up a tasty mixture of vegetables in a spicy, creamy sauce with crisp filo pastry. It makes a perfect dish for a special family supper.

SERVES 4
1 onion, chopped
2 carrots, coarsely grated
1 zucchini, chopped
12 oz potatoes, chopped
5 tbsp butter
2 tsp mild curry paste
½ tsp dried thyme
⅔ cup water
salt and ground black pepper
1 egg, beaten
2 tbsp light cream
½ cup Cheddar cheese, grated
8 sheets filo pastry
sesame seeds, to sprinkle

1 Fry the onion, carrots, zucchini and potatoes in half the butter for 5 minutes until they are soft, then add the curry paste and cook for a further minute.

2 Add the thyme, water and seasoning. Continue to cook gently, uncovered for another 10 minutes.

3 Allow the mixture to cool and mix in the egg, cream and cheese. Chill until ready to fill and roll.

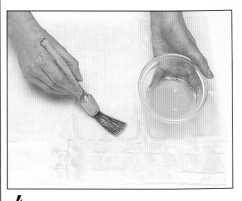

4 Melt the remaining butter and lay out four sheets of filo pastry, slightly overlapping them to form a fairly large rectangle. Brush with butter and fit the other sheets on top. Brush again.

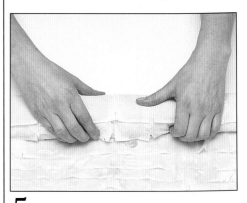

5 Spoon the filling along one long edge, then roll up the pastry. Form it into a circle and brush again with the last of the butter. Sprinkle over the sesame seeds and set on a baking sheet.

6 Heat the oven to 375°F, then bake the strudel for about 25 minutes until golden and crisp. Allow to stand for 5 minutes or so before cutting.

Coronation Salad

This famous salad dressing was created especially for the coronation dinner of Queen Elizabeth II. It is a wonderful accompaniment to eggs and vegetables.

SERVES 6
1 lb new potatoes
salt
3 tbsp vinaigrette dressing
3 scallions, chopped
ground black pepper
6 eggs, hard-boiled and halved
frilly lettuce leaves, to serve
¼ cucumber, sliced then cut in shreds
6 large radishes, sliced
1 bunch watercress
DRESSING
2 tbsp olive oil
1 small onion, chopped
1 tbsp mild curry powder or korma
  spice mix
2 tsp tomato paste
2 tbsp lemon juice
2 tbsp sherry
1¼ cups mayonnaise
¼ pint natural yogurt

1 Boil the potatoes in salted water until tender. Drain them and then toss them in the vinaigrette dressing.

2 Allow the potatoes to cool, stirring in the scallions and seasoning. Cool the mixture thoroughly.

3 Meanwhile, make the coronation dressing. Heat the oil and fry the onion for 3 minutes until it is soft. Stir in the spice powder and fry for a further minute. Mix in all the other dressing ingredients.

4 Stir the dressing into the potatoes, add the eggs then chill. Line a serving platter with lettuce leaves and pile the salad in the center. Scatter over the cucumber, radishes and watercress.

Pasta and Wild Mushroom Casserole

Bake pasta shapes in a golden crumb coating layered with a rich bechamel sauce and mushrooms. Superb!

SERVES 4–6
7 oz pasta shapes
2½ cups milk
1 bay leaf
small onion stuck with 6 cloves
4 tbsp butter
3 tbsp fresh bread crumbs
2 tsp dried mixed herbs
⅓ cup all-purpose flour
4 tbsp Parmesan cheese, freshly grated
fresh nutmeg, grated
salt and ground black pepper
2 eggs, beaten
1 × ½ oz package dried porcini or cep mushrooms
12 oz button mushrooms, sliced
2 garlic cloves, crushed
2 tbsp olive oil
2 tbsp fresh parsley, chopped

1 Boil the pasta according to the instructions on the package. Drain and set aside. Heat the milk with the bay leaf and clove-studded onion and stand for 15 minutes. Remove the bay leaf and onion.

2 Melt the butter in a saucepan and use a little to brush the inside of a large oval casserole. Mix the crumbs and mixed herbs together and use them to coat the inside of the dish.

3 Stir the flour into the butter, cook for a minute then slowly add the hot milk to make a smooth sauce. Add the cheese, nutmeg, seasoning and cooked pasta. Cool for 5 minutes then beat in the eggs.

4 Soak the porcini or cep mushrooms in a little hot water until soft. Reserve the liquor and chop the mushrooms.

5 Fry the porcinis or ceps with the button mushrooms and garlic in the oil for 3 minutes. Season, stir in the liquor and reduce down. Add the parsley.

6 Spoon a layer of pasta into the dish. Sprinkle over the mushrooms then more pasta and so on, finishing with pasta. Cover with greased foil. Heat the oven to 375°F and bake for about 25–30 minutes. Allow to stand for 5 minutes before turning out to serve.

Eggplant Boats

These can be prepared ahead and baked prior to eating. The hazelnut topping contrasts nicely with the smooth eggplant filling.

SERVES 4
⅔ cup brown basmati rice
2 medium size eggplants, halved lengthwise
1 onion, chopped
2 garlic cloves, crushed
1 small green pepper, chopped
4 oz mushrooms, sliced
3 tbsp olive oil
3 oz Cheddar cheese, grated
1 egg, beaten
½ tsp marjoram
salt and ground black pepper
2 tbsp hazelnuts, chopped

1 Boil the rice according to the instructions on the package, drain and then cool. Scoop out the flesh from the eggplants and chop. Blanch the shells in boiling water for 2 minutes, then drain upside down.

2 Fry the eggplant flesh, onion, garlic, pepper and mushrooms in the oil, for about 5 minutes.

3 Mix in the rice, cheese, egg, marjoram and seasoning. Arrange the eggplant shells in an ovenproof dish. Spoon the filling inside. Sprinkle over the nuts. Chill until ready to bake.

4 Heat the oven to 375°F and bake the eggplants for about 25 minutes until the filling is set and the nuts are golden brown in color.

Grilled Vegetables with Salsa

Enjoy a barbecue with these chunky grilled vegetables. Serve hot with a no-cook salsa.

SERVES 4
1 large sweet potato, cut in thick slices
2 zucchini, halved lengthwise
salt
2 red peppers, quartered
olive oil, to brush
SALSA
2 large tomatoes, skinned and finely chopped
2 scallions, finely chopped
1 small green chili, chopped
juice of 1 small lime
2 tbsp fresh coriander, chopped
salt and ground black pepper

1 Par boil the sweet potato for 5 minutes until it is barely tender. Drain thoroughly and leave to cool.

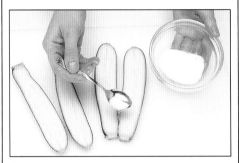

2 Sprinkle the zucchini with a little salt and leave to drain in a colander for 20 minutes, then pat dry.

3 Make the salsa by mixing all the ingredients together, and allow them to stand for about 30 minutes to mellow.

4 Prepare the barbecue until the coals glow, or preheat a broiler. Brush the potato slices, zucchini and peppers with oil and cook them until they are lightly charred and softened, brushing with oil again and turning at least once. Serve hot accompanied by the salsa.

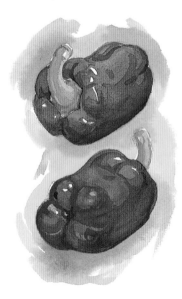

Garden Vegetable Terrine

Perfect for a special family picnic or buffet, this is a softly set, creamy terrine of colorful vegetables wrapped in glossy spinach leaves. Select large, really fresh spinach leaves for the best results.

SERVES 6
8 oz fresh leaf spinach, well washed
3 carrots, cut in sticks
3–4 long, thin leeks
4 oz long green beans, topped and tailed
1 red pepper, cut in strips
2 zucchini, cut in sticks
4 oz broccoli florets
SAUCE
1 egg and 2 yolks
1¼ cups light cream
fresh nutmeg, grated
1 tsp salt
2 oz Cheddar cheese, grated
oil, for greasing
ground black pepper

1 Blanch the spinach quickly in boiling water, then drain, refresh in cold water and drain again. Take care not to break up the leaves, then carefully pat them dry.

2 Grease a 2 lb loaf pan and line the base with a sheet of waxed paper. Line the pan with the spinach leaves, trimming any thick stalks. Allow the leaves to overhang the sides of the pan.

3 Blanch the rest of the vegetables in boiling, salted water until just tender. Drain and refresh in cold water then, when completely cool, pat dry with pieces of paper towel.

4 Place the vegetables into the loaf pan in a colorful mixture, making sure the sticks of vegetables lie lengthwise.

5 Beat the sauce ingredients together and slowly pour over the vegetables. Tap the loaf pan to ensure the sauce seeps into the gaps. Fold over the spinach leaves at the top of the terrine.

6 Cover the terrine with a sheet of greased foil, then bake in a roasting pan half full of boiling water at 350°F for about 1–1¼ hours until set.

7 Cool the terrine in the pan, then chill. To serve, loosen the sides and shake gently out. Serve cut in thick slices.

Crêpe Galette

Make a stack of light crêpes and then layer them together with a tasty lentil filling for an impressive dinner party main course. Serve with a home made tomato sauce.

SERVES 6
1 cup all-purpose flour
good pinch of salt
1 egg
1¼ cups buttermilk, or milk and
  water, mixed
oil, for cooking
FILLING
2 leeks, thinly sliced
1 small fennel bulb, thinly sliced
4 tbsp olive oil
¾ cup red lentils
⅔ cup dry white wine
1 × 14 oz can chopped tomatoes
1¼ cups stock
1 tsp dried oregano
salt and ground black pepper
1 onion, sliced
8 oz mushrooms, sliced
8 oz frozen leaf spinach, thawed and
  squeezed dry
7 oz low fat cream cheese
2 oz Parmesan cheese, freshly grated

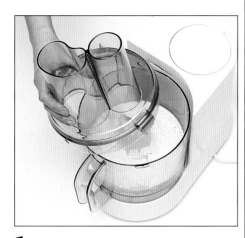

1 Make the crêpe batter by mixing the flour, salt, egg and buttermilk or milk and water in a blender until smooth. Set aside while you prepare the filling.

2 Gently fry the leeks and fennel in half the olive oil for 5 minutes, then add the lentils and wine. Cook for a minute until reduced down, then stir in the tomatoes and stock.

3 Bring the leek/fennel mixture to a boil, add the oregano and seasoning then simmer for 20 minutes, stirring it occasionally until it thickens.

4 Fry the onion and mushrooms in the remaining olive oil for 5 minutes, stir in the spinach and heat. Season well, then mix in the cream cheese.

5 Make about 12–14 crêpes with the batter in a well heated non-stick frying pan. Lightly grease an 8 in round deep spring-form cake pan and line the base and sides with some of the crêpes, overlapping them as necessary.

6 Layer the remaining crêpes with the two fillings, sprinkling Parmesan in between and pressing them down well. Finish with a crêpe on top.

7 Cover with foil and set aside to rest. Preheat the oven to 375°F. Bake for about 40 minutes, then turn out carefully and allow to firm up for 10 minutes before cutting into wedges.

COOK'S TIP

This can be frozen ready made up, but it is probably nicer if frozen in parts – the crêpes interleaved with waxed paper and then wrapped in foil, and the sauce frozen separately.

Polenta Fingers with Beans and Tomatoes

Polenta, or cornmeal, is a popular family favorite in Italy. It is eaten either hot from a bowl or allowed to set, cut into fingers, and grilled.

SERVES 6
7½ cups milk and water, mixed
2 tsp salt
1½ cups polenta
2 tbsp butter, plus extra for spreading
2 oz Parmesan cheese, freshly grated
ground black pepper
SAUCE
1 onion, chopped
2 garlic cloves, crushed
2 tbsp olive oil
1 × 14 oz can chopped tomatoes
salt and ground black pepper
good pinch of dried sage
8 oz frozen broad beans

1   In a large saucepan, bring the milk and water to a boil. Stir in the salt. While stirring with a wooden spoon trickle the polenta into the boiling liquid in a steady stream and continue stirring until the mixture has thickened.

2   Lower the heat and simmer for about 20 minutes, stirring frequently. Add the butter, cheese and seasoning.

3   Lightly grease a shallow roasting pan and pour in the polenta mixture. Cool, then chill overnight.

4   For the sauce, fry the onion and garlic in the oil for 5 minutes. Add the tomatoes, seasoning and sage and cook for a further 10 minutes. Stir in the broad beans and cook for 5 minutes more.

5   Turn out the polenta and cut into fingers. Grill both sides until brown and crisp. Spread with a little butter and serve accompanied by the tomato and beans.

Paprika and Parmesan Tartlets

Pretty pink pastry tarts with a tangy cream filling are ideal for handing round at cocktail parties. Make the shells ahead of the party and fill them just before serving.

MAKES 18
2 cups all-purpose flour
2 tsp paprika
10 tbsp butter or sunflower margarine
scant ½ cup Parmesan cheese, freshly grated
cold water, to bind
FILLING
12 oz goat cheese
2 oz arugula leaves, or watercress, chopped
2 tbsp fresh chives, chopped
salt and ground black pepper
1 lb tomatoes, sliced

1   Sift the flour with the paprika and rub in the butter or margarine. Stir in the Parmesan and mix to a firm dough with cold water.

2   Roll out the pastry and stamp out 18 rounds, large enough to fit into muffin pans. Prick the bases well with a fork, press them into the muffin pans and chill while you preheat the oven to 375°F.

3   Bake the tartlets for 15 minutes until crisp. Cool them on a wire rack.

4   Beat the cheese with the arugula or watercress, chives and seasoning. Slice the tomatoes, allowing roughly two slices per tart.

5   When ready to serve, spoon the filling into the tarts. Top each one with some tomato and garnish with extra arugula or watercress leaves.

Tofu Satay

Grill cubes of tofu until crispy, then serve with a Thai-style peanut sauce. Soaking the sticks helps them withstand the hot broiling.

SERVES 4–6
2 × 7 oz packages smoked tofu
3 tbsp light soy sauce
2 tsp sesame oil
1 garlic clove, crushed
1 yellow and 1 red pepper, cut in squares
8–12 fresh bay leaves
sunflower oil, for grilling
SAUCE
2 scallions, finely chopped
2 garlic cloves, crushed
good pinch chili powder or few drops hot chilli sauce
1 tsp granulated sugar
1 tbsp white vinegar
2 tbsp light soy sauce
3 tbsp crunchy peanut butter

1 Soak 8–12 wooden satay sticks in water for 20 minutes, then drain. Cut the tofu into bite-sized cubes and mix with the soy sauce, sesame oil and garlic. Cover and marinate for 20 minutes.

2 Beat the sauce ingredients together until well blended. Avoid using a food processor for this as the texture should be slightly chunky.

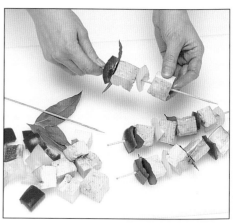

3 Drain the tofu and thread the cubes onto the soaked sticks with the pepper squares and bay leaves. Larger leaves may need to be halved.

4 Heat a broiler or barbecue until quite hot. Brush the satays with oil. Broil, turning the sticks occasionally, until the ingredients are browned and crisp. Serve hot with the dipping sauce.

Party Mousakka

Always a popular favorite for both guests and the cook at parties, mousakka is ideal because it benefits from being made ahead of time, requiring just reheating on the day.

SERVES 8
2 large eggplants, thinly sliced
6 zucchini, cut in chunks
⅔ cup olive oil, plus extra if required
1½ lb potatoes, thinly sliced
2 onions, sliced
3 garlic cloves, crushed
⅔ cup dry white wine
2 × 14 oz cans chopped tomatoes
2 tbsp tomato paste
1 × 15 oz can green lentils
2 tsp dried oregano
4 tbsp chopped fresh parsley
2 cups feta cheese, crumbled
salt and ground black pepper
BECHAMEL SAUCE
3 tbsp butter
4 tbsp all-purpose flour
2½ cups milk
2 eggs, beaten
4 tbsp freshly grated Parmesan cheese
nutmeg, freshly grated

1 Lightly salt the eggplants and zucchini in a colander and leave them to drain for 30 minutes. Rinse and pat dry.

2 Heat the oil until quite hot in a frying pan and quickly brown the eggplant and zucchini slices. Remove them with a slotted spoon and drain on a paper towel. This step is important to cut down on the oiliness of the eggplant. Next, brown the potato slices, remove and pat dry. Add the onion and garlic to the pan with a little extra oil, if required, and fry until lightly browned – about 5 minutes.

3 Pour in the wine and cook until reduced down then add the tomatoes and lentils plus the liquor from the can. Stir in the herbs and season well. Cover and simmer for 15 minutes.

4 In a large ovenproof dish, layer the vegetables, trickling the tomato and lentil sauce in between and scattering over the feta cheese. Finish off with a layer of eggplant slices.

5 Cover the vegetables with a sheet of foil and bake at 375°F for 25 minutes or until the vegetables are quite soft but not overcooked.

6 Meanwhile, for the bechamel sauce, put the butter, flour and milk into a saucepan all together and bring slowly to a boil, stirring or whisking constantly. It should thicken and become smooth. Season and add the nutmeg.

7 Remove the sauce and cool for 5 minutes then beat in the eggs. Pour it over the eggplant and sprinkle with the Parmesan. If cooking ahead, cool and chill at this stage.

8 To finish, return to the oven uncovered and bake for a further 25–30 minutes until golden and bubbling hot.

Basmati and Green Lentil Salad

Puy lentils from France (sometimes known as green lentils) are small, deliciously nutty pulses, highly prized by gourmets. They blend beautifully with aromatic basmati rice.

SERVES 6
⅔ cup puys de dome (green) lentils, soaked
1¼ cups basmati rice, rinsed well
2 carrots, coarsely grated
⅓ cucumber, halved, seeded and coarsely grated
3 scallions, sliced
3 tbsp fresh parsley, chopped
DRESSING
2 tbsp sunflower oil
2 tbsp extra virgin olive oil
2 tbsp wine vinegar
2 tbsp fresh lemon juice
good pinch of granulated sugar
salt and ground black pepper

1 Soak the lentils for 30 minutes. Meanwhile, make the dressing by shaking all the ingredients together in a screw-topped jar. Set aside.

2 Boil the lentils in plenty of unsalted water for 20–25 minutes or until soft. Drain thoroughly.

3 Boil the basmati rice for 10 minutes, then drain.

4 Mix together the rice and lentils in the dressing and season well. Leave to cool.

5 Add the carrots, cucumber, scallions and parsley. Spoon into an attractive serving bowl and chill before serving.

Wild Rice with Julienne Vegetables

Make an accompanying dish more interesting with some exquisite wild rice. For the best flavor, buy a good quality wild rice (which is actually a cereal!) and, to shorten the cooking time, soak it overnight.

SERVES 4
½ cup wild rice
1 red onion, sliced
2 carrots, cut in julienne sticks
2 celery stalks, cut in julienne sticks
4 tbsp butter
⅔ cup stock or water
salt and ground black pepper
2 medium zucchini, cut in thicker sticks
a few toasted almond flakes, to serve

1 Drain the soaked rice, then boil in plenty of unsalted water for 15–20 minutes, until it is soft and many of the grains have burst open. Drain.

2 In another saucepan, gently fry the onion, carrots and celery in the butter for 2 minutes, then pour in the stock or water and season well.

3 Bring to a boil, simmer for 2 minutes then stir in the zucchini. Cook for 1 more minute then mix in the rice. Reheat and serve hot sprinkled with the almonds.

Oven-Crisp Asparagus Rolls

A lovely treat when fresh asparagus is in season is to wrap blanched spears in slices of thin bread and bake in a buttery glaze until crisp. Out of season, use canned or frozen spears.

SERVES 8
8 thick spears of fresh asparagus
salt
8½ tbsp butter, softened
1 tbsp coarse grained mustard
grated rind of 1 lemon
ground black pepper
8 slices thin white bread, crusts removed

1 Trim the asparagus stalks, peeling the tough woody skin at the base. Blanch until just tender in a shallow pan of boiling, salted water. Drain and refresh in cold water. Pat dry.

2 Blend two-thirds of the butter with the mustard, lemon rind and seasoning. Spread over the slices of bread.

3 Lay an asparagus spear on the edge of each bread slice and roll it up tightly. Place the rolls join side down on a lightly greased baking sheet.

4 Melt the remaining butter and brush over the rolls. Heat the oven to 375°F and bake for 12–15 minutes until golden and crisp. Cool slightly before serving.

VARIATION

Asparagus has always been something of a luxury as its season is so short, but imports from across the world means that it is available almost all year round, albeit at a price!

Thin baby asparagus, known as sprue, can be eaten raw in salads or stir-fried quickly. Opinions differ about the merits of green or white asparagus spears. The latter are forced in the dark (hence their white color), but some people consider them to have a better flavor and texture.

Ratatouille Tart

Serve this pretty tart warm so the cheese is easy to cut and eat. For the best results, make the base and filling separately then combine and heat just before serving.

SERVES 6
1 cup all-purpose flour
¾ cup whole wheat flour
1 tsp dried mixed herbs
salt and ground black pepper
½ cup sunflower margarine
3–4 tbsp cold water
FILLING
1 small eggplant, thickly sliced
salt
3 tbsp olive oil
1 onion, sliced
1 red or yellow pepper, sliced
2 garlic cloves, crushed
2 zucchini, thickly sliced
2 tomatoes, skinned and sliced
ground black pepper
2 tbsp fresh basil, chopped
5 oz Mozzarella cheese, sliced
2 tbsp pine nuts

1 Mix the two flours with the herbs and seasoning then rub in the margarine until it resembles fine crumbs. Mix to a firm dough with water.

2 Roll out the pastry and line a 9 in round pie pan. Prick the base, line with foil and baking beans then allow to rest in the fridge.

3 Meanwhile, sprinkle the eggplant lightly with salt and leave to drain for 30 minutes in a colander. Rinse and pat dry.

4 Heat the oil in a frying pan and fry the onion and pepper for 5 minutes, then add the garlic, zucchini and eggplant. Fry for a further 10 minutes, stirring the mixture occasionally.

5 Stir in the tomatoes and seasoning, cook for a further 3 minutes, add the basil then remove the pan from the heat and allow to cool.

6 Heat the oven to 400°F. Place the tart shell on a baking sheet and bake for 25 minutes, removing the foil and baking beans for the last 5 minutes. Cool and then, if possible, carefully remove the case from the pan.

7 When ready to serve, spoon the vegetables into the case using a slotted spoon so any juices drain off and don't soak into the pastry. Top with the cheese slices and pine nuts. Toast under a preheated broiler until golden and bubbling. Serve warm.

Filo Baskets with Ginger Dill Vegetables

Make up some elegant filo baskets, then fill them with crisply steamed vegetables tossed in an interesting and tasty sauce.

SERVES 4
4 sheets of filo pastry
3 tbsp butter, melted
FILLING
2 tbsp olive oil
1 tbsp fresh root ginger, grated
2 garlic cloves, crushed
3 shallots, sliced
8 oz wild mushrooms, sliced
4 oz oyster mushrooms, sliced
1 zucchini, sliced
7 oz sour cream
2 tbsp fresh dill, chopped
salt and ground black pepper
dill and parsley sprigs, to serve

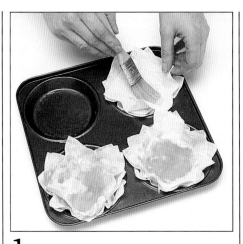

1 Cut the filo sheets into four. Line four large muffin pans, angling the layers so that the corners form a pretty star shape. Brush between each layer with butter. Set aside.

2 Heat the oven to 375°F. Bake the shells for about 10 minutes until golden brown and crisp. Remove and cool.

3 For the filling, heat the oil and sauté the ginger, garlic and shallots for 2 minutes, then add the mushrooms and zucchini. Cook for another 3 minutes.

4 Mix in the sour cream, chopped dill and seasoning. Heat until just bubbling then spoon into the filo cases. Garnish with the dill and parsley and serve.

Gado Gado Salad with Peanut Sambal

Indonesians enjoy a salad of lightly steamed vegetables topped with a peanut sauce. It is ideal for a colorful summer buffet dish.

SERVES 6
8 oz new potatoes, halved
2 carrots, cut in sticks
4 oz green beans
½ small cauliflower, broken into florets
¼ firm white cabbage, shredded
7 oz bean or lentil sprouts
4 eggs, hard-boiled and quartered
bunch watercress, trimmed
SAUCE
6 tbsp crunchy peanut butter
1¼ cups cold water
1 garlic clove, crushed
2 tbsp dark soy sauce
1 tbsp dry sherry
2 tsp superfine sugar
1 tbsp fresh lemon juice
1 tsp anchovy paste

1 Fit a steamer or metal colander over a pan of gently boiling water. Cook the potatoes for 10 minutes.

2 Add the rest of the vegetables and sprouts and steam for a further 10 minutes until tender. Cool and arrange on a platter with the egg quarters surrounded by the watercress.

3 Beat all the sauce ingredients together until smooth. Put the sauce in a small bowl and drizzle over each individual serving of salad.

Persian Rice and Lentils with a Tahdeeg

Persian or Iranian cuisine is an exotic and delicious one, steeped in history. Flavors are intense and exotic, and somehow more sophisticated than other Mediterranean styles. A tahdeeg is the glorious, golden rice crust that forms at the bottom of the saucepan.

SERVES 8

1 lb basmati rice, rinsed thoroughly and soaked
2 onions, 1 chopped, 1 thinly sliced
2 garlic cloves, crushed
⅔ cup sunflower oil
1 cup green lentils, soaked
2½ cups stock
⅓ cup raisins
2 tsp ground coriander
3 tbsp tomato paste
salt and ground black pepper
few strands of saffron
1 egg yolk, beaten
2 tsp natural yogurt
6 tbsp butter, melted and strained
extra oil, for frying

1 Boil the rinsed and drained rice in plenty of well salted water for 3 minutes only. Drain again.

2 Meanwhile, fry the chopped onion and garlic in 2 tbsp of oil for 5 minutes, then add the lentils, stock, raisins, coriander, tomato paste and seasoning. Bring to a boil, then cover and simmer for 20 minutes. Set aside.

3 Soak the saffron strands in a little hot water. Remove about 8 tbsp of the rice and mix with the egg yolk and yogurt. Season well.

4 In a large saucepan, heat about two-thirds of the remaining oil and scatter the egg and yogurt rice evenly over the base.

5 Scatter the remaining rice into the pan, alternating it with the lentils. Build up in a pyramid shape away from the sides of the pan, finishing with plain rice on top.

6 With a long wooden spoon handle, make three holes down to the bottom of the pan and drizzle over the butter. Bring to a high heat, then wrap the pan lid in a clean, wet dish towel and place firmly on top. When a good head of steam appears, turn the heat down to low. Cook for about 30 minutes.

7 Meanwhile, fry the sliced onion in the remaining oil until browned and crisp. Drain well and set aside.

8 Remove the rice pan from the heat, still covered and stand it briefly in a sink of cold water for a minute or two to loosen the base. Remove the lid and mix a few spoons of the white rice with the saffron water prepared in Step 3.

9 Toss the rice and lentils together in the pan and spoon out onto a serving dish in a mound. Scatter the saffron rice on top. Break up the rice crust on the bottom (the prized tahdeeg) and place around the mound. Scatter the onions on top of the saffron rice and serve.

Vegetable Fritters with Tzatziki

Spicy deep-fried eggplant and zucchini slices served with a creamy yogurt and dill dip make a good, simple party starter or an excellent side dish.

SERVES 4–6
½ cucumber, coarsely grated
8 oz natural yogurt
1 tbsp extra virgin olive oil
2 tsp fresh lemon juice
2 tbsp fresh dill, chopped
1 tbsp fresh mint, chopped
1 garlic clove, crushed
salt and ground black pepper
1 large eggplant, thickly sliced
2 zucchini, thickly sliced
1 egg white, beaten
4 tbsp all-purpose flour
2 tsp ground coriander
ground cumin

1 For the dip, mix the cucumber, yogurt, oil, lemon juice, dill, mint, garlic and seasoning. Spoon into a bowl then set aside.

2 Layer the eggplant and zucchini in a colander and sprinkle them with salt. Leave for 30 minutes. Rinse well in cold water, and then pat dry.

3 Put the egg white into a bowl. Mix the flour, coriander and cumin with seasoning and put into another bowl.

4 Dip the vegetables first into the egg white then into the seasoned flour and set aside.

5 Heat about 1 in of oil in a deep frying pan until quite hot, then fry the vegetables a few at a time until they are golden in color and crisp.

6 Drain and keep warm while you fry the remainder. Serve warm on a platter with a bowl of the tzatziki dip lightly sprinkled with paprika.

Mushroom Saucers

Recipes which are already portioned are a great boon for the host, as guests can help themselves without feeling they are taking more than their fair share. Large flat mushrooms are great for this reason.

SERVES 8
8 large flat mushrooms with stalks removed, wiped clean and chopped
3 tbsp olive oil
salt and ground black pepper
1 onion, sliced
1 tsp cumin seeds
1 lb leaf spinach, well washed, stalks trimmed, and shredded
1 × 15 oz can red kidney beans, drained
7 oz soft cheese with garlic and herbs
2 medium tomatoes, halved, seeded and sliced in strips

1 Heat the oven to 375°F. Lightly grease a large, shallow ovenproof dish. Brush the mushrooms with some oil, place them in the dish and season well with salt and pepper. Cover with foil and bake for about 15–20 minutes. Uncover, drain and reserve the juices.

3 Stir in the spinach and fry until the leaves begin to wilt, then mix in the beans and heat well. Add the cheese, stirring until melted and season again.

2 Fry the onion and chopped mushroom stalks in the remaining oil for 5 minutes until soft. Then add the cumin seeds and mushroom juices and cook for a minute longer until reduced down.

4 Divide the mixture between the mushroom cups and return to the oven to heat through. Serve garnished with tomato slices.

Birds' Nests

A recipe from an old hand-written cookbook dated 1887. These are also known as Welsh Eggs because they resemble Scotch Eggs but they have leeks in the filling. They are ideal for taking on picnics.

SERVES 6
6 eggs, hard-boiled
all-purpose flour for dredging, seasoned
    with salt and paprika
1 leek, chopped
2 tsp sunflower oil
2 cups fresh white breadcrumbs
grated rind and juice of 1 lmeon
½ cup vegetarian shredded suet
4 tbsp fresh parsley, chopped
1 tsp dried thyme
salt and ground black pepper
1 egg, beaten
½ cup dried breadcrumbs
oil, for deep fat frying
lettuce and tomato slices, to garnish

1 Peel the hard-boiled eggs and toss in the seasoned flour.

2 Fry the leeks in the oil for about 3 minutes. Remove, cool, then mix with the fresh breadcrumbs, lemon rind and juice, suet, herbs and seasoning. If the mixture is somewhat dry add a little water.

3 Shape the mixture around the eggs, then toss first into the beaten egg, then the dried breadcrumbs. Set aside on a plate to chill for 30 minutes.

4 Pour enough oil to fill one-third of a deep fat fryer and heat to a temperature of 375°F, and fry the eggs, three at a time, for about 3 minutes. Remove and drain on paper towel.

5 Serve, cool, cut in half on a platter lined with lettuce and garnished with tomato slices.

Portable Salads

A clever Victorian notion for transporting saucy salads neatly to a picnic site was to pack them in a hollowed out loaf of bread.

SERVES 6
1 large, deep crusty loaf of bread
softened butter or margarine, for
  spreading
few leaves of crisp lettuce
4 eggs, hardboiled and chopped
12 oz new potatoes, boiled and sliced
1 green pepper, thinly sliced
2 carrots, coarsely grated
3 scallions, chopped
4 oz Gouda cheese, grated
salt and ground black pepper
DRESSING
2 tbsp mayonnaise
2 tbsp natural yogurt
2 tbsp milk
1 garlic clove, crushed (optional)
1 tbsp fresh dill, chopped

1 Cut the top from the loaf and scoop out the bread inside. Use this for making fresh bread crumbs and freeze for later.

2 Spread the inside of the loaf lightly with the softened butter or margarine, then line with the lettuce leaves.

3 Mix the eggs with the vegetables and cheese. Season well. Beat the dressing ingredients together and mix into the egg and vegetables.

4 Spoon the dressed salad into the hollow and lined loaf, replace the lid and wrap in plastic wrap. Chill until ready to transport. To serve, spoon the salad onto plates and cut the crust into chunks.

Marbled Quails' Eggs

Hard-boiled quails' eggs re-boiled in smoky China tea assume a pretty marbled skin. It's quite a treat to dip them into a fragrant spicy salt and hand them round with drinks. Szechuan peppercorns can be bought from Oriental food stores.

SERVES 4–6
12 quails' eggs
2½ cups strong brewed lapsang souchong tea
1 tbsp dark soy sauce
1 tbsp dry sherry
2 star anise pods
lettuce leaves, to serve
ground Szechuan red peppercorns
sea salt, to mix

1 Place the quails' eggs in cold water and bring to a boil. Time them for 2 minutes from when the water boils.

2 Remove the eggs from the pan and run them under cold water to cool. Tap the shells all over so they are crazed, but do not peel yet.

3 In a saucepan, bring the tea to the boil and add the soy sauce, sherry and star anise. Re-boil the eggs for about 15 minutes, partially covered, so the liquid does not boil dry.

4 Cool the eggs, then peel them and arrange on a small platter lined with lettuce leaves. Mix the ground red peppercorns with equal quantities of salt and place in a small side dish.

Beet Roulade

This roulade is simple to make, yet will create a stunning impression. Ideally, prepare it in the fall when beets are at their best.

SERVES 6
8 oz fresh beets, cooked and peeled
½ tsp ground cumin
2 tbsp butter
2 tsp grated onion
4 eggs, separated
salt and ground black pepper
FILLING
⅔ cup sour cream or heavy cream
2 tsp white wine vinegar
good pinch dry mustard powder
1 tsp sugar
3 tbsp fresh parsley, chopped
2 tbsp fresh dill, chopped
3 tbsp horseradish relish

1 Line a jelly roll pan with waxed paper and then grease the paper. Preheat the oven to 375°F.

2 Roughly chop the beets, then blend to a purée in a food processor and beat in the cumin, butter, onion, egg yolks and seasoning. Turn the beet purée into a large bowl.

3 In another bowl, that is spotlessly clean, whisk the egg whites until they form soft peaks. Fold them into the beet mixture carefully.

4 Spoon the mixture into the jelly roll pan, level and bake for about 15 minutes until just firm to touch.

5 Have ready a clean dish towel laid over a wire rack. Turn the beet mixture out onto the towel, and remove the paper carefully in strips.

6 Beat the sour cream or cream until lightly stiff, then fold in the remaining ingredients. Spread this mixture onto the beet mixture. Roll up the roulade very carefully and allow it to cool.

Pan Bagna

You need three essential elements for this French picnic classic: a really fresh French baguette, ripe juicy tomatoes, full of flavor and good, extra virgin olive oil. It is ideal to pack for a picnic.

SERVES 3–4
1 long French baguette, split in half
1 garlic clove, halved
4–6 tbsp extra virgin olive oil
3–4 ripe tomatoes, thinly sliced
salt and ground black pepper
1 small green pepper, thinly sliced
2 oz Gruyère cheese, thinly sliced
a few pitted black olives, sliced
6 fresh basil leaves

1 Rub the cut surface of the bread with the garlic and discard the clove. Brush over half of the olive oil on both halves of the bread.

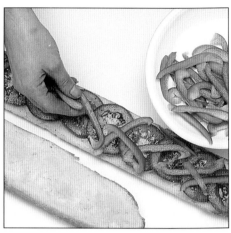

2 Lay the tomato slices on top, season well and top with the pepper. Drizzle over the remaining oil.

3 Top the tomatoes with the cheese slices, olives and basil leaves. Sandwich the loaf together firmly and wrap it in plastic wrap for an hour or more. Serve cut diagonally in thick slices.

Sandwiches, Rolls and Fillings

There is an increasing variety of wonderful breads and rolls now for the picnic packer to choose from – not only variations on white and whole wheat breads, but also flavored breads such as onion, walnut, tomato swirl and black olive. Make sure the breads are fresh and spread them right up to the edges using good butter or a quality margarine spread. Once filled, wrap in plastic wrap and chill until required. However, many a good sandwich is spoiled if served too cold, so allow it to return to room temperature before eating.

FILLING IDEAS
Unless specified, keep the fillings in separate layers rather than mixing the ingredients together.

☐ De-rinded Brie or Camembert, mixed with chopped walnuts or pecans and served with frisé or curly endive lettuce.

☐ Yeast extract, scrambled egg (made without milk) and bean sprout (especially good with alfalfa sprouts). Spread the bread or roll with yeast extract rather than mixing it into the egg.

☐ Fry onions in olive oil until crisp and brown. Cool. Layer with shredded, young raw spinach leaves and grated cheese mixed with a little mayonnaise.

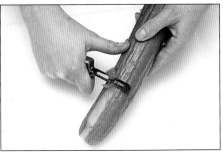

☐ **Real English Cucumber Sandwiches.** Peel strips from a whole cucumber to leave it stripy, then slice thinly on a mandoline or a food processor slicer. Sprinkle lightly with salt and leave to drain for 30 minutes in a colander. Pat dry. Sprinkle lightly with a little vinegar and black pepper. Sandwich in very fresh white or whole wheat bread and cut off the crusts. Cut into small triangles.

Pasta and Beet Salad

Color is vital at a party table, and this salad is certainly eye catching. Serve the egg and avocado at the last moment to avoid discoloration.

SERVES 8
2 uncooked beets, scrubbed
8 oz pasta shells or twists
3 tbsp vinaigrette dressing
salt and ground black pepper
2 celery stalks, thinly sliced
3 scallions, sliced
⅔ cup walnuts or hazelnuts, roughly
  chopped
1 dessert apple, cored, halved and sliced
DRESSING
4 tbsp mayonnaise
3 tbsp natural yogurt or ricotta cheese
2 tbsp milk
2 tsp horseradish relish
TO SERVE
curly lettuce leaves
3 eggs, hard boiled and chopped
2 ripe avocadoes
bunch watercress

1 Boil the beets, without peeling them, in lightly salted water until they are just tender. Drain, cool, peel and chop, then set aside.

2 Cook the pasta according to the instructions on the package, then drain and toss in the vinaigrette and season well. Cool. Mix the pasta with the beet, celery, onions, nuts and apple.

3 Stir all the dressing ingredients together and mix into the pasta bowl. Chill well.

4 To serve, line a pretty salad bowl with the lettuce leaves and pile the salad in the center. When ready to serve, scatter over the chopped egg. Peel and slice the avocadoes and arrange them on top, then sprinkle over the watercress.

Gazpacho

This classic Spanish no-cook soup is ideal for taking on picnics as it can be packed straight from the refrigerator. Keep the chopped vegetables in separate pots and hand them round as an accompaniment.

SERVES 6
1 slice white bread, crust removed
cold water, to soak
1 garlic clove, crushed
2 tbsp extra virgin olive oil
2 tbsp white wine vinegar
6 large ripe tomatoes, skinned and finely
  chopped
1 small onion, finely chopped
½ tsp paprika
good pinch ground cumin
⅔ cup tomato juice
salt and ground black pepper
TO GARNISH
1 green pepper, chopped
⅓ cucumber, peeled, seeded and
  chopped
CROÛTONS
2 slices bread, cubed and deep fried

1 Soak the bread slice in enough cold water just to cover and leave for about 5 minutes, then mash with a fork.

2 Pound the garlic, oil and vinegar with a pestle and mortar or blend in a food processor. Mix this into the bread.

3 Spoon the mixture into a bowl and stir in the tomatoes, onion, spices and tomato juice. Season well and store in the refrigerator. Prepare the garnishes and store these in separate containers.

4 For a picnic, pour the chilled soup into a flask. Otherwise, pour into a chilled glass salad bowl and hand the garnishes round in smaller bowls.

Sesame Egg Roll

A Japanese-inspired idea. A thin omelet is rolled up with a creamy watercress filling and served cut in thick slices.

SERVES 3–4
3 eggs
1 tbsp soy sauce
1 tbsp sesame seeds
1 tsp sesame seed oil
salt and ground black pepper
1 tbsp sunflower oil
3 oz cream cheese with garlic
1 bunch watercress, chopped

1 Beat the eggs with the soy sauce, sesame seeds, sesame seed oil and seasoning.

2 Heat the sunflower oil in a large frying pan until quite hot, then pour in the egg mixture, tilting the pan so it covers the whole base. Cook until firm.

3 Allow the omelet to stand in the pan for a few minutes then turn out onto a chopping board and cool completely.

4 Beat the cream cheese until soft, season well then mix in the chopped watercress. Spread this over the omelet, then roll it up quite firmly. Wrap in plastic wrap and chill.

Homemade Coleslaw

Forget store-bought coleslaw! Making your own at home is quite quick and easy to do – and it tastes fresh, crunchy and wonderful.

SERVES 4–6
¼ firm white cabbage
1 small onion, finely chopped
2 celery stalks, thinly sliced
2 carrots, coarsely grated
1–2 tsp caraway seeds (optional)
1 dessert apple, cored and chopped
  (optional)
½ cup walnuts, chopped (optional)
salt and ground black pepper
DRESSING
3 tbsp mayonnaise
2 tbsp light cream or natural yogurt
1 tsp lemon rind, grated
salt and ground black pepper

1 Cut and discard the core from the cabbage quarter then shred the leaves finely. Place this in a large bowl.

2 Into the cabbage toss the onion, celery and carrot, plus the caraway seeds, apple and walnuts, if using. Season well.

3 Mix the dressing ingredients together and stir into the vegetables. Cover and allow to stand for 2 hours, stirring occasionally, then chill the coleslaw lightly before serving.

Malfatti with Red Sauce

If you ever felt dumplings were a little heavy, try making these light Italian spinach and ricotta malfatti instead. Serve them with a simple tomato and red pepper sauce.

SERVES 4–6
1 lb fresh leaf spinach, well washed, stalks trimmed
1 small onion, chopped
1 garlic clove, crushed
1 tbsp olive oil
14 oz ricotta cheese
⅔ cup dried bread crumbs
½ cup all-purpose flour
1 tsp salt
2 oz Parmesan cheese, freshly grated
fresh nutmeg, grated, to taste
3 eggs, beaten
2 tbsp butter, melted
SAUCE
1 large, red pepper, chopped
1 small red onion, chopped
2 tbsp olive oil
1 × 14 oz can chopped tomatoes
⅔ cup water
good pinch dried oregano
salt and ground black pepper
2 tbsp light cream

1 Blanch the spinach in the tiniest amount of water until it is limp, then drain well, pressing it through a sieve with the back of a ladle or spoon. Chop very finely.

COOK'S TIP

Quenelles are oval-shaped dumplings. To shape the malfatti into quenelles you need two dessert spoons. Scoop up the mixture with one spoon, making sure it is mounded up, then, using the other spoon, scoop the mixture off the first spoon, twisting the top spoon into the bowl of the second.

Repeat this action two or three times until the quenelle is smooth, and then gently knock it off onto a plate ready to cook.

2 Lightly fry the onion and garlic in the oil for 5 minutes then mix with the spinach together with the ricotta cheese, bread crumbs, flour, salt, most of the Parmesan and nutmeg.

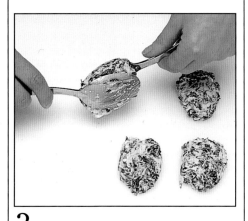

3 Allow the mixture to cool, add the eggs and melted butter, then mold into 12 small "sausage" shapes.

4 Meanwhile, make the sauce by lightly sautéeing the pepper and onion in the oil for 5 minutes. Add the tomatoes, water, oregano and seasoning. Bring to a boil, then simmer for 5 minutes.

5 When cooked, remove from the heat and blend to a purée in a food processor. Return to the pan, then stir in the cream. Check the seasoning.

6 Bring a shallow pan of salted water to a gentle boil and drop the malfatti into it a few at a time and poach them for about 5 minutes. Drain them well and keep them warm.

7 Arrange the malfatti on warm plates and drizzle over the sauce. Serve topped with the remaining Parmesan.

Curried Mango Chutney Dip

A quickly made, tangy and spicy dip or dressing, ideal as a dip for strips of pitta bread, grissini or sticks of fresh chopped vegetables.

SERVES 4–6
1 onion, chopped
1 garlic clove, crushed
2 tbsp sunflower oil
2 tsp mild curry powder
8 oz natural yogurt
2 tbsp mango chutney
salt and ground black pepper
2 tbsp fresh parsley, chopped

1 Gently fry the onion and garlic in the oil for 5 minutes until they are soft. Add the curry powder and cook for a further minute then allow the mixture to cool.

2 Spoon into a food processor with the yogurt, chutney and seasoning and blend until smooth.

3 Stir in the parsley and chill before serving with a variety of vegetable crudités and strips of bread.

Nutty Mushroom Paté

Spread this delicious, medium-texture paté on chunks of crusty French bread and eat with crisp leaves of lettuce and sweet cherry tomatoes.

SERVES 4–6
1 onion, chopped
1 garlic clove, crushed
1 tbsp sunflower oil
2 tbsp water
1 tbsp dry sherry
8 oz button mushrooms, chopped
salt and ground black pepper
¾ cup cashew nuts or walnuts, chopped
5 oz low fat farmer's cheese
1 tbsp soy sauce
few dashes Worcestershire sauce
fresh parsley, chopped, and a little paprika, to serve

1 Gently fry the onion and garlic in the oil for 3 minutes then add the water, sherry and mushrooms. Cook, stirring for about 5 minutes. Season to taste and allow to cool a little.

2 Put the mixture into a food processor with the nuts, cheese and sauces. Blend to a rough purée – do not allow it to become too smooth.

3 Check the seasoning, then spoon into a serving dish. Swirl the top and serve lightly chilled sprinkled with parsley and paprika.

Antipasti with Aioli

For a simple starter or hand-around cocktail canapé, make a bowl of the classic French/Spanish garlic sauce – aioli – and serve it with a selection of attractively prepared vegetables and breads.

SERVES 4–6
4 garlic cloves
2 egg yolks
½ tsp salt
ground black pepper
1¼ cups flavorful extra virgin olive oil
TO SERVE
red or yellow pepper, cut in thick strips
fennel, cut in slivers
radishes, halved if large
button mushrooms
broccoli florets
grissini sticks
French bread, thinly sliced

1 Crush the garlic into a bowl then beat in the egg yolks, salt and some ground black pepper.

2 Stand the bowl on a damp cloth and slowly trickle in the oil, drip by drip, whisking with a balloon whisk until you have a thick, creamy sauce. As the sauce thickens, you can add the oil in slightly larger amounts.

3 Spoon the aioli into a bowl. Arrange the dipping food around the bowl and serve lightly chilled.

Camembert Fritters

A popular snack to pass around at cocktail parties. These deep-fried cheeses are quite simple to do. They are served with a red onion marmalade which can be made in advance and stored in the refrigerator.

SERVES 4
MARMALADE
2 lb red onions, sliced
3 tbsp sunflower oil
3 tbsp olive oil
1 tbsp coriander berries, crushed
2 large bay leaves
3 tbsp granulated sugar
6 tbsp red wine vinegar
2 tsp salt
CHEESE
8 individual portions of Camembert
1 egg, beaten
1 cup plain white or whole wheat dried
   bread crumbs, to coat
oil, for deep fat frying

1 Make the marmalade first. In a large saucepan, gently fry the onions in the oil, covered, for 20 minutes or so or until they are soft.

2 Add the remaining marmalade ingredients, stir well and cook, uncovered, for a further 10–15 minutes until most of the liquid has been absorbed. Cool and then set aside.

VARIATION

You could make these fritters with fingers of firm Brie, or try it using baby rounds of goat cheese.

3 Prepare the cheese by first scratching the mold rind lightly with a fork. Dip first in egg then in bread crumbs to coat well. Dip and coat a second time if necessary. Store on a plate.

4 Pour oil into a deep fat fryer so it is one-third full; heat to 375°F.

5 Carefully lower the coated cheeses into the hot oil three or four at a time and fry until golden and crisp, about 2 minutes or less.

6 Drain well on paper towel and fry the rest, reheating the oil in between. Serve hot with some of the marmalade.

DESSERTS & BREADS

Freshly baked breads, cakes and fruit-filled desserts are all utterly irresistible. Here you can also find traditional treats to make Christmas extra special.

Zucchini Crown Bread

Adding grated zucchini and cheese to a loaf mixture will keep it tasting fresher for longer. This is a good loaf to serve with a bowl of special soup.

SERVES 8
1 lb zucchini, coarsely grated
salt
5 cups all-purpose flour
2 packages fast action yeast
4 tbsp Parmesan cheese, freshly grated
ground black pepper
2 tbsp olive oil
lukewarm water, to mix
milk, to glaze
sesame seeds, to garnish

1 Spread out the zucchini in a colander and sprinkle lightly with salt. Leave to drain for 30 minutes, then pat dry.

2 Mix the flour, yeast and Parmesan together and season with black pepper.

3 Stir in the oil and zucchini and add enough lukewarm water to give you a good firm dough.

4 Knead the dough on a lightly floured surface until it is smooth, then return it to the mixing bowl, cover it with oiled plastic wrap and leave it to rise in a warm place.

5 Meanwhile, grease and line a 9 in round cake pan, and then preheat the oven to 400°F.

6 When the dough has doubled in size, turn it out of the bowl, punch it down and knead it lightly. Break into eight balls, rolling each one and placing them in the tin as shown. Brush the tops with milk and sprinkle over the sesame seeds.

7 Allow to rise again, then bake for 25 minutes or until golden brown. Cool slightly in the pan, then turn out the bread to cool further.

Rosemary Focaccia

Italian flat bread is becoming increasingly popular and is easy to make using packaged bread mix. Add traditional ingredients like olives and sun-dried tomatoes.

SERVES 4
1 lb package white bread mix
4 tbsp extra virgin olive oil
2 tsp dried rosemary, crushed
8 sun-dried tomatoes, snipped
12 black olives, pitted and chopped
¾ cup lukewarm water
sea salt flakes

VARIATION

If you want to make your own bread instead of using a bread mix, then use a packet of easy-blend yeast for each 6 cups of flour. Mix the yeast and flour together then add the remaining ingredients as per the recipe.

1 Mix the bread mix with half the oil, the rosemary, tomatoes, olives and water until it forms a firm dough.

2 Turn out the dough onto a lightly floured surface and knead thoroughly for 5 minutes. Return the dough to the mixing bowl and cover with a piece of oiled plastic wrap.

3 Leave the dough to rise in a warm place until it has doubled in size. Meanwhile, lightly grease two baking sheets with olive oil and preheat the oven to 425°F.

4 Turn out the risen dough, punch down and knead again. Divide into two and shape into rounds. Place on the baking sheet, and punch hollows in the dough. Trickle over the remaining olive oil and sprinkle with salt.

5 Bake the focaccia for 12–15 minutes until golden brown and cooked. Slide off onto wire racks to cool. Eat slightly warm.

Brown Soda Bread

This is very easy to make – all you have to do is simply mix and bake. Instead of yeast, baking soda and cream of tartar are the rising agents. This is an excellent recipe for those new to bread making.

MAKES ONE 2 LB LOAF
4 cups all-purpose flour
3 cups whole wheat flour
2 tsp salt
1 tbsp baking soda
4 tsp cream of tartar
2 tsp superfine sugar
4 tbsp butter
up to 3¾ cups buttermilk or skimmed milk
extra whole wheat flour, to sprinkle

1 Lightly grease a baking sheet. Preheat the oven to 375°F.

2 Sift all the dry ingredients into a large bowl, tipping any bran from the flour back into the bowl.

3 Rub the butter into the flour mixture, then add enough buttermilk or milk to make a soft dough. You may not need all of it, so add it cautiously.

4 Knead lightly until smooth then transfer to the baking sheet and shape to a large round about 2 in thick.

5 Using the floured handle of a wooden spoon, form a large cross on top of the dough. Sprinkle over a little extra whole wheat flour.

6 Bake for 40–50 minutes until risen and firm. Cool for 5 minutes before transferring to a wire rack to cool further.

Cardamom and Saffron Tea Loaf

An aromatic sweet bread ideal for afternoon tea, or lightly toasted for breakfast. Use the packages of fast action or easy blend yeasts, they make bread making so simple.

MAKES ONE 2 LB LOAF
good pinch saffron strands
3 cups lukewarm milk
2 tbsp butter
8 cups all-purpose flour
2 packages fast action yeast
1½ oz superfine sugar
6 cardamom pods, split open and seeds
   extracted
⅔ cup raisins
2 tbsp honey
1 egg, beaten

1 Crush the saffron into a cup containing a little of the warm milk and leave to infuse for 5 minutes.

2 Rub the butter into the flour then mix in the yeast, sugar and cardamom seeds (these may need rubbing to separate them). Stir in the raisins.

3 Beat the remaining milk with the honey and egg, then mix this into the flour along with the saffron milk and strands, stirring well until a firm dough is formed. You may not need all the milk: it depends on the flour.

4 Turn out the dough and knead it on a lightly floured board for about 5 minutes until smooth.

5 Return the dough to the mixing bowl, cover with oiled plastic wrap and leave in a warm place until doubled in size. This could take between 1–3 hours.

VARIATION

For simplicity, leave out the saffron and cardamom and replace with 2 tsp ground cinnamon.

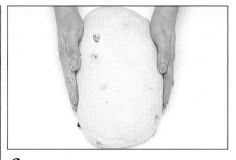

6 Turn the dough out onto a floured board again, punch it down, knead for 3 minutes then shape it into a fat roll and fit it into a greased loaf pan.

7 Cover with a sheet of lightly oiled plastic wrap and stand in a warm place until the dough begins to rise again. Preheat the oven to 400°F.

8 Bake the loaf for 25 minutes until golden brown and firm on top. Turn out of the pan and as it cools brush the top with honey. Slice when cold and spread with butter. It is also good lightly toasted.

Dinner Milk Rolls

Making bread especially for your dinner guests is not only a wonderful gesture, it is also quite easy to do. You can vary the shapes of the rolls too.

MAKES 12–16
4 cups all-purpose flour
2 tsp salt
2 tbsp butter
1 package easy-blend fast action yeast
scant 2 cups lukewarm milk
extra cold milk, to glaze
poppy, sesame and sunflower seeds or sea salt flakes, to garnish

1 Sift the flour and salt into a large bowl or food processor. Rub in or blend in the butter, then mix in the yeast.

2 Mix to a firm dough with the milk, adding it cautiously if the dough is a little dry in case you don't need it all.

3 Knead for at least 5 minutes by hand, or for 2 minutes in a food processor. Place in a bowl, cover with oiled plastic wrap and leave to rise until doubled in size.

4 Turn out of the bowl, punch down and knead again, then break off into 12–16 pieces and either roll each one into a round or make into fun shapes.

5 Place on an oiled baking sheet, glaze the tops with extra milk and sprinkle over seeds or sea salt flakes of your choice.

6 Leave to start rising again, while you preheat the oven to 450°F. Bake the rolls for 12 minutes or until golden brown and cooked. Leave to cool on a wire rack. Eat as soon as possible, as homemade bread stales quickly.

Indian Pan-fried Breads

Instead of yeast, this dough uses baking soda as a rising agent. Traditional Indian spices add a tasty bite to the bread.

MAKES ABOUT 24
2 cups whole wheat flour
2 cups all-purpose flour
1 tsp salt
1 tsp sugar
2 tsp baking soda
2 tsp cumin seeds
2 tsp black mustard seeds
1 tsp fennel seeds
1 lb natural yogurt
6 tbsp vegetable ghee or clarified butter
5 tbsp sunflower oil

1 Mix the flours with the salt, sugar, baking soda and spices. Mix to a firm dough with the yogurt, being sure to add the yogurt in gradual amounts, as you may not need it all.

2 If the dough is too dry, add cold water slowly until you achieve the correct consistency. Cover and chill for 2 hours.

3 Divide the dough into 24 pieces and roll each piece out to a thin round. Stack the rounds under a clean dish towel as you roll out the rest.

4 Fry the breads in the hot ghee or butter and oil, starting with a quarter and adding more ghee/butter and oil each time you fry. Drain the breads well on kitchen paper towel and store under the dish towel. Serve with curries and raitas.

Rich Chocolate Cake

A simple all-in-one cake sandwiched with a simple but very delicious ganache icing. It makes a particularly good special-occasion cake.

SERVES 6–8
1 cup self-rising flour
3 tbsp cocoa
1 tsp baking powder
10 tbsp butter, softened, or sunflower margarine
¾ cup superfine sugar
3 eggs, beaten
2 tbsp water
ICING
5 oz dark (plain) chocolate
⅔ cup heavy cream
1 tsp vanilla extract
2 tbsp apricot or raspberry jam

1 Grease and line a deep 8 in round cake pan with waxed paper, and then preheat the oven to 325°F.

2 Put all the cake ingredients into a large bowl or food processor. Beat very well with a wooden spoon or blend in the food processor until the mixture is smooth and creamy.

3 Spoon into the cake pan and bake for about 40–45 minutes or until risen and springy to the touch. Cool upside down on a wire rack for 15 minutes, then turn out and set aside to cool completely.

4 To make the icing, break the chocolate into a heatproof bowl and pour in the cream and vanilla extract. Melt in a microwave on full power for 2–3 minutes, or over a pan of simmering water.

5 Cool the icing, stirring it occasionally and chill lightly until it thickens. Split the cake in half. Spread the jam on one half and half the icing on top of that.

6 Sandwich the two halves together and spread the rest of the icing on top, swirling it attractively or marking it with the tip of a table knife. Decorate as desired with candies or candles – even edible flowers can add a nice touch.

Passion Cake

So called because this is a cake associated with Passion Sunday. The carrots and banana give the cake a rich, moist texture.

SERVES 6–8
1¾ cups self-rising flour
2 tsp baking powder
1 tsp cinnamon
½ tsp fresh nutmeg, grated
10 tbsp butter, softened, or sunflower margarine
¾ cup soft brown sugar
grated rind of 1 lemon
2 eggs, beaten
2 carrots, coarsely grated
1 ripe banana, mashed
¾ cup raisins
½ cup walnuts or pecans, chopped
2 tbsp milk
FROSTING
7 oz cream cheese, softened
1½ oz confectioners' sugar
juice of 1 lemon
grated rind of 1 orange
6–8 walnuts, halved
coffee crystal sugar, to sprinkle

1 Grease and line a deep 8 in cake pan with waxed paper. Preheat the oven to 350°F. Sift the flour, baking powder and spices into a bowl.

2 Using an electric mixer, cream the butter and sugar with the lemon rind until it is light and fluffy, then beat in the eggs. Fold in the flour mixture, then the carrots, banana, raisins, nuts and milk.

3 Spoon the mixture into the prepared pan, level the top and bake for about 1 hour until it is risen and the top is springy to touch. Turn the pan upside down and allow the cake to cool in the pan for 30 minutes. Turn onto a wire rack.

4 When cold, split the cake in half. Cream the cheese with the confectioners' sugar, lemon juice and orange rind, then sandwich the two halves together with half of the frosting.

5 Spread the rest of the frosting on top, swirling it attractively. Decorate with the walnut halves and sprinkle with the coffee crystal sugar.

Yogurt with Apricots and Pistachios

If you allow a thick yogurt to drain overnight, it becomes even thicker and more luscious. Add honeyed apricots and nuts and you have an exotic yet simple dessert.

SERVES 4
1 lb yogurt
⅔ cup no-need-to-soak natural dried apricots, snipped
1 tbsp honey
orange rind, grated
2 tbsp unsalted pistachios, roughly chopped
ground cinnamon

VARIATION

For a simple dessert, strain the fruit, cover with yogurt and sprinkle with brown sugar and a little allspice or cinnamon.

1 Place the yogurt in a fine sieve and allow it to drain overnight in the fridge over a bowl.

2 Discard the whey from the yogurt. Place the apricots in a saucepan, barely cover with water and simmer for just 3 minutes, to soften. Drain and transfer to a bowl, then mix with the honey.

3 Mix the yogurt with the apricots, orange rind and nuts. Spoon into sundae dishes, sprinkle over a little cinnamon and chill.

Fresh Pineapple Salad

Very refreshing, this salad can be prepared ahead. Orange flower water is available from Middle Eastern food stores or good delicatessens.

SERVES 4
1 small ripe pineapple
confectioners' sugar, to taste
1 tbsp orange flower water, or more if liked
good ½ cup fresh dates, pitted and quartered
8 oz fresh strawberries, sliced
few fresh mint sprigs, to serve

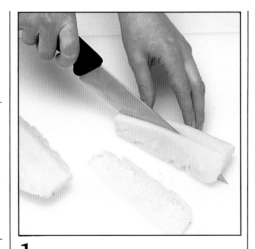

1 Cut the skin from the pineapple and, using the tip of a vegetable peeler, remove as many brown 'eyes' as possible. Quarter lengthways, remove the core then slice.

2 Lay the pineapple in a shallow, pretty glass bowl. Sprinkle with sugar and orange flower water.

3 Add the dates and strawberries to the pineapple, cover and chill for a good 2 hours, stirring once or twice. Serve lightly chilled decorated with a few mint sprigs.

Walnut and Raspberry Meringue

Make sure you beat the egg whites stiffly to form a good firm foam for the meringue. When you fold in the nuts the meringue will hold its shape. Assemble this dish just before serving, if at all possible.

SERVES 4–6
3 egg whites
few drops of fresh lemon juice
1 cup superfine sugar
¾ cup walnuts, finely chopped
1 lb fresh raspberries
¾ cup sour cream or heavy cream
few drops vanilla extract
confectioners' sugar, to taste

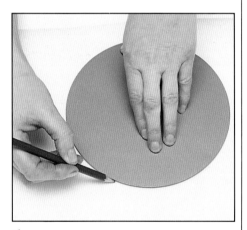

1 Preheat the oven to 325°F. Draw three 8 in circles on non-stick parchment paper. Place the circles on baking sheets.

COOK'S TIP

Don't waste egg whites if you have recipes which call for yolks only. They do freeze very well and can be stored in batches of 3 or 4 whites at a time. In fact, when thawed, frozen egg whites make a much better foam.

2 Whisk the egg whites in a spotlessly clean and grease-free bowl with the few drops of lemon juice. (This gives a more stable foam).

3 When the whites are softly stiff, gradually whisk in the sugar until thick and glossy. Quickly and carefully fold in the nuts.

4 Spread or pipe the mixture onto the three paper circles. Bake for 40–50 minutes until firm and crisp on top. This may have to be done in batches.

5 Cool on a wire rack and peel off the paper. Store in an airtight container until ready to serve.

6 Whip the sour cream or cream with the vanilla and sugar, until the mixture is quite stiff.

7 Reserve a few raspberries for decoration, crush those remaining and mix into the creamy cheese mixture.

8 Spread the fruit cream on the three meringues. Sandwich them together and decorate the top layer with the reserved raspberries.

Rum-Baked Bananas

This is a quick, hot dessert which bakes in just minutes. When cooked, bananas have a really full flavor that is enhanced by rum and orange. Serve this dish with a trickle of cream.

SERVES 4
4 bananas
grated rind and juice of 1 orange
2 tbsp dark rum
¼ cup soft brown sugar (optional)
good pinch of ground ginger
fresh nutmeg, grated
3 tbsp butter

1 Preheat the oven to 350°F. Peel the bananas and then slice them into four large ramekins.

2 Spoon the orange juice and rum over the sliced bananas. Sprinkle over the sugar, if using, orange rind and spices. Dot with butter.

3 Cover the ramekins with small pieces of foil or buttered waxed paper and bake for 15 minutes. Allow to cool slightly before serving with cream or yogurt.

Muesli Bars

Instead of buying expensive crunchy oat bars, bake your own. They are much nicer and really quite easy to make. Use muesli with no added sugar for the bars.

MAKES 12–16
4 cups muesli
5 tbsp sunflower oil
5 tbsp honey
1 tsp mixed spice
1 egg, beaten
1½ oz dark brown sugar (optional)

COOK'S TIP

To make your own muesli, buy bags of flaked grains and oats from your local health food store. As these will make a large amount, you need to make sure you eat a lot of muesli! Choose jumbo rolled oats, barley flakes and wheat flakes, then add a selection of seeds, dried fruits and nuts.

1 Preheat the oven to 325°F. Grease and line a shallow baking pan measuring about 7 × 11 in.

2 Mix all the ingredients together and spoon into the pan, patting the mixture until it is level.

3 Bake for 30–35 minutes until light brown round the edges. Remove, cool slightly then mark into 12–16 pieces.

4 Cool completely, turn out onto a wire rack and break into the marked pieces. Store in an airtight container.

Oatmeal and Date Brownies

These brownies are marvelous for special brunches or as a tea time treat. The secret of chewy, moist brownies is not to overcook them.

MAKES 16
5 oz dark (plain) chocolate
4 tbsp butter
¾ cup rolled oats
3 tbsp wheat germ
⅓ cup milk powder
½ tsp baking powder
½ tsp salt
½ cup walnuts, chopped
⅓ cup dates, chopped
¼ cup dark brown sugar
1 tsp vanilla extract
2 eggs, beaten

1 Break the chocolate into a heatproof bowl and add the butter. Melt it either in a microwave on full power for 2 minutes, stirring once, or in a pan over very gently simmering water.

2 Cool the chocolate, stirring it occasionally. Grease and line an 8 in square cake pan with waxed paper, then preheat the oven to 350°F.

3 Combine all the dry ingredients together in a bowl then beat in the melted chocolate, vanilla and eggs.

4 Pour the mixture into the prepared cake pan, level the top and bake for about 20–25 minutes until it is firm around the edges yet still soft in the center.

5 Cool the brownies in the pan, then chill. When they are more solid, turn them out of the pan and cut into 16 squares. Store in an airtight container.

COOK'S TIP

These make a marvelous lunch box or picnic snack, and if you store them for a day or two before eating they will become more moist and even more chewy.

Cut-and-Come-Again Fruit Cake

A rich fruit cake keeps well for quite some time so it is ideal to have one on hand for when you feel like a slice of something sweet or when guests drop in unexpectedly.

SERVES 8–10
2 sticks butter, softened, or sunflower
   margarine
1 cup soft brown sugar
4 eggs, beaten
1 tbsp black molasses
3 cups all-purpose flour
1 tsp cinnamon
3 tbsp milk
2 lb dried mixed fruit (e.g. raisins,
   currants, cherries)
½ cup flaked almonds
grated rind of 1 lemon
a few blanched almond halves (optional)
a little milk, to glaze (optional)
2 tbsp brandy or rum (optional)

1 Preheat the oven to 275°F. Grease and line a deep 8 in cake pan with doubled waxed paper.

2 Cream the butter or margarine and sugar until light and fluffy. Beat in the eggs with the molasses and stir into the creamed mixture.

3 Sift the flour and spice and fold this into the mixture, alternating it with the milk. Stir in the dried fruit, almonds and lemon rind.

4 Spoon the mixture into the prepared pan. If liked, dip the almond halves in a little milk and arrange them on top.

5 Bake on a shelf one position below the center of the oven for about 3 hours. When cooked, the top of the cake will feel quite firm and a skewer inserted into the center will come out clean.

6 Allow the cake to cool for 10 minutes then, if using the brandy or rum, make small holes in the top of the cake with a thin skewer. Slowly pour the liquor over the cake.

7 Allow the cake to cool completely in the pan, then turn it out and remove the paper. Wrap it in clean waxed paper and foil or store in an airtight container for one week before cutting.

Thai Rice Cake

A celebration gâteau made from fragrant Thai rice covered with a tangy cream icing. Top with fresh berry fruits or pipe on a greeting in melted chocolate. This is a good cake to serve to those with a gluten allergy as it is flour free.

SERVES 8–10
1¼ cups Thai fragrant or Jasmine rice
4½ cups milk
¾ cup superfine sugar
6 cardamom pods, crushed open
2 bay leaves
1¼ cups whipping cream
6 eggs, separated
TOPPING
1¼ cups heavy cream
7 oz cream cheese
1 tsp vanilla extract
grated rind of 1 lemon
1½ oz superfine sugar
soft berry fruits and sliced star or kiwi
   fruits, to decorate

1 Grease and line a deep 10 in round cake pan. Boil the rice in unsalted water for 3 minutes then drain.

2 Return the rice to the pan with the milk, sugar, cardamom and bay leaves. Bring to a boil, then lower the heat and simmer the mixture for 20 minutes, stirring it occasionally.

3 Allow the mixture to cool, then remove the bay leaves and any cardamom husks. Turn the mixture into a bowl. Beat in the cream and then the egg yolks. Preheat the oven to 350°F.

VARIATION

If you prefer something simpler, turn the cake out and top with sliced fruits or a lovely tumble of berries and pitted cherries. Serve the topping separately, thinning it down slightly with a little milk.

4 Whisk the egg whites until they are softly stiff and fold into the rice mixture. Spoon into the prepared pan and bake for 45–50 minutes until risen and golden brown. The center should be slightly wobbly – it will firm up as it cools.

5 Chill overnight in the pan. Turn out on to a serving plate. Whip the heavy cream until stiff then mix in the cream cheese, vanilla, lemon rind and sugar.

6 Cover the top and sides of the cake with the cream, swirling it attractively. Decorate with soft berry fruits and sliced star or kiwi fruits.

Apple and Apricot Crumble

Lightly cook the fruit base first for the best results. That way you'll get a delicious contrast between soft fruit and crunchy topping.

SERVES 4–6
1 × 15 oz can apricot halves in natural juice
1 lb cooking apples, peeled and sliced
granulated sugar, to taste (optional)
grated rind of 1 orange
fresh nutmeg, grated
TOPPING
1¾ cups all-purpose flour
½ cup rolled oats
10 tbsp butter or sunflower margarine
¼ cup soft brown sugar
light brown sugar, to sprinkle

1 Preheat the oven to 375°F. Drain the apricot halves, reserving a little of the natural juice.

2 Put the apples into a saucepan with a little of the reserved apricot juice and sugar to taste. Simmer for just 5 minutes to cook the fruit lightly.

3 Transfer the apples into an ovenproof pie dish and stir in the apricots, orange rind and nutmeg to taste.

4 Rub the flour, oats and butter or margarine together until they form fine crumbs. (You can use a food processor if you prefer.) Mix in the soft brown sugar.

5 Scatter the crumble over the fruit, spreading it evenly. Sprinkle with a little brown sugar. Bake for about 30 minutes until golden and crisp on top. Allow to cool slightly before serving.

French Apple Cake

With its moist texture and fruity flavor, this cake is ideal to serve as a dessert accompanied by a little cream or yogurt.

SERVES 6–8
1 lb cooking apples or tart dessert apples, cored and chopped
1 cup self-rising flour
1 tsp baking powder
⅔ cup superfine sugar
6 tbsp milk
4 tbsp butter, melted
3 eggs
1 tsp fresh nutmeg, grated
TOPPING
6 tbsp butter, softened, or sunflower margarine
½ cup superfine sugar
1 tsp vanilla extract
sifted confectioners' sugar, to dust

1 Preheat the oven to 325°F. Grease and line the base of a deep 9 in round cake pan with waxed paper.

2 Put the chopped apples into the base of the cake pan.

3 Put all the remaining cake ingredients, except 1 egg, into a bowl or food processor. Beat to a smooth batter.

4 Pour the batter over the apples in the pan, level the top then bake for 40–45 minutes until lightly golden.

5 Meanwhile, cream the topping ingredients together with the remaining egg. Remove the cake from the oven and spoon over the topping.

6 Return the cake to the oven for a further 20–25 minutes until it is golden brown. Cool the cake in the pan, then turn it out and finish with a light dusting of confectioners' sugar.

VARIATION

We don't use fresh fruit very often in cake mixtures, which is a pity as it gives a delightful flavor. Try adding finely chopped pears or pineapple, or even raspberries.

Chocolate and Lemon Cream

What better excuse to add iron to your diet than by eating some good dark chocolate? Contrast the richness with tangy sour cream and yogurt.

SERVES 4
5 oz dark (plain) chocolate
3 tbsp water
1 tbsp rum or brandy (optional)
grated rind of 1 lemon
3½ oz sour cream
3½ oz natural yogurt
TO DECORATE
kumquats, sliced
sprigs of mint

COOK'S TIP

If you heat chocolate too quickly or fiercely, the cocoa solids will "seize" and go lumpy and nothing can then be done to make a smooth all-chocolate sauce.

1 Break up the chocolate into a heatproof bowl. Add the water and either melt very slowly over a pan of gently simmering water or in a microwave on full power for 2–2½ minutes.

2 Stir well until smooth and allow the chocolate to cool for 10 minutes. Stir in the spirit, if using, and the lemon rind, yogurt and sour cream.

3 Spoon into four elegant wine glasses and chill until set. Decorate with kumquats and sprigs of mint.

Orange, Honey and Mint Terrine

Very refreshing and easy to make, this is an ideal dessert to serve after a rich meal as it is a good palate cleanser.

SERVES 6
8–10 oranges
2½ cups fresh orange juice
2 tbsp honey
4 tsp agar-agar
3 tbsp fresh mint, chopped
mint leaves to decorate (optional)

1 Grate the rind from two oranges and put this aside. Cut the peel and membrane from all the oranges, then slice each one thinly, removing any pips, and saving any juice.

2 Heat the orange juice (plus any saved) with the honey, reserved rind and agar-agar. Stir the mixture until it dissolves.

3 Pack the orange slices into a 2 lb loaf pan, sprinkling the mint in between. Slowly pour over the hot orange juice. Tap the pan lightly so that all the juice settles.

4 Chill the terrine overnight, if possible, until it is quite firm. When ready to serve, dip the pan briefly into very hot water and turn the terrine out to a wet platter. Decorate with more mint leaves, if you wish. Serve cut into thick slices.

Halva

The Greeks love home made halva which they cook in a saucepan with semolina, olive oil, sugar, honey and almonds. You can either eat it warm, or allow it to set and cut it into slices or squares.

MAKES 12–16 PIECES
2 cups granulated sugar
4½ cups water
2 cinnamon sticks
1 cup olive oil
3 cups semolina
¾ cup blanched almonds, 6–8 halved, the rest chopped
½ cup honey
ground cinnamon, to serve

1 Reserve 4 tbsp sugar and dissolve the rest in the water over a gentle heat, stirring from time to time.

2 Add the cinnamon sticks, bring to a boil then simmer for 5 minutes. Cool and remove the cinnamon sticks.

3 Heat the olive oil in a large heavy-based saucepan and, when it is quite hot, stir in the semolina. Cook, stirring occasionally, until it turns a golden brown, then add the chopped almonds and cook for a further minute or so.

4 Keep the heat low and stir in the syrup, taking care as the semolina may spit. Bring the mixture to a boil, stirring it constantly. When it is just smooth, remove the pan from the heat and stir in the honey.

5 Cool slightly and mix in the reserved sugar. Pour the halva into a greased and lined shallow pan, pat it down and mark into squares.

6 Sprinkle the halva lightly with ground cinnamon and fix one almond half on each square. When set, cut up and serve.

Rice Condé Sundae

Cook a rice pudding on top of the stove instead of in the oven for a light creamy texture which is particularly good served cold topped with fruits, toasted nuts and even a trickle of hot chocolate sauce.

SERVES 4
⅓ cup pudding rice
2½ cups milk
1 tsp vanilla extract
½ tsp ground cinnamon
1½ oz granulated sugar
TO SERVE
Choose from: strawberries, raspberries or
   blueberries
chocolate sauce
flaked toasted almonds

1 Put the rice, milk, vanilla extract, cinnamon and sugar into a medium-sized saucepan. Bring to a boil, stirring constantly, and then turn down the heat to a gentle simmer.

2 Cook the rice for about 30–40 minutes, stirring occasionally. Add extra milk if it reduces down too quickly.

3 Make sure the grains are soft, then remove the pan from the heat and allow the rice to cool, stirring it occasionally. When cold, chill the rice in the refrigerator.

4 Just before serving, stir the rice and spoon into four sundae dishes. Top with fruits, chocolate sauce and almonds.

VARIATION

Milk puddings are at last enjoying something of a comeback in popularity. Instead of simple pudding rice try using a Thai fragrant or Jasmine rice for a delicious natural flavor. For a firmer texture, an Italian Arborio rice makes a good pudding too.

There's no need to use a lot of high-fat milk or cream either. A pudding made with low fat or even fat-free milk can be just as nice and is much more healthy.

Pear and Hazelnut Flan

A delicious flan for Sunday lunch. Ground hazelnuts are increasingly easier to find, but if you have difficulty, then either grind your own or use ground almonds instead.

SERVES 6–8
1 cup all-purpose flour
¾ cup whole wheat flour
3 tbsp cold water
8 tbsp sunflower margarine
FILLING
½ cup self-rising flour
1 cup ground hazelnuts
1 tsp vanilla extract
2 oz superfine sugar
4 tbsp butter, softened
2 eggs, beaten
3 tbsp raspberry jam
1 × 14 oz can pears in natural juice
a few chopped hazelnuts, to decorate

1 Stir the flours together in a large mixing bowl, then rub in the margarine until it resembles fine crumbs. Mix to a firm dough with the water.

2 Roll out the pastry and use it to line a 9–10 in pie pan, pressing it firmly up the sides after trimming, so the pastry sits above the pan a little. Prick the base, line with waxed paper and fill with baking beans. Chill for 30 minutes.

3 Preheat the oven to 400°F. Place the pie pan on a baking sheet and bake for 20 minutes, removing the paper and beans for the last 5 minutes.

4 Meanwhile, beat all the filling ingredients together except for the jam and pears. If the mixture is a little thick, stir in some of the pear juice.

5 Reduce the oven temperature to 350°F. Spread the jam on the pastry base and spoon over the filling.

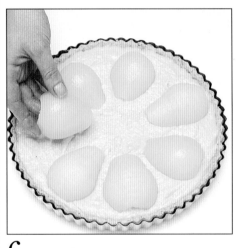

6 Drain the pears well and arrange them cut side down in the filling. Scatter over the nuts and bake for 30 minutes until risen, firm and golden brown.

VARIATION

This is also good made with ground almonds and canned apricots or pineapple pieces. For chocaholics, add 2 tbsp cocoa powder to the flour in the filling (and even to the pastry if you want to make it richer and more chocolatey) plus a little grated lemon rind. Instead of raspberry jam, you could use chocolate spread and top with the pears in the recipe.

Three-fruits Compôte

Mixing dried fruits with fresh ones makes a good combination, especially if flavored delicately with a little orange flower water. A melon-ball scoop gives the compôte a classy touch, but you could simply chop the melon into cubes.

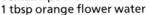

SERVES 6
1 cup no-need-to-soak dried apricots
1 small ripe pineapple
1 small ripe melon
1 tbsp orange flower water

1 Put the apricots into a saucepan with ½ pint water. Bring to a boil, then simmer for 5 minutes. Leave to cool.

2 Peel and quarter the pineapple then cut the core from each quarter and discard. Cut the flesh into chunks.

3 Seed the melon and scoop balls from the flesh. Save any juices which fall from the fruits and tip them into the apricots.

4 Stir in the orange flower water and mix all the fruits together. Pour into an attractive serving dish and chill lightly before serving.

VARIATION

A good fruit salad needn't be a boring mixture of multi-colored fruits swimming in sweet syrup. Instead of the usual apple, orange and grape type of salad, give it a theme, such as red berry fruits or a variety of sliced green fruits – even a dish of just one fruit nicely prepared and sprinkled lightly with some sugar and fresh lemon juice can look beautiful and tastes delicious. Do not use more than three fruits in a salad so that the flavors remain distinct.

Red Berry Tart with Lemon Cream Filling

Just right for warm summer days, this tart is best filled just before serving so the pastry remains mouth-wateringly crisp. Select a range of red berry fruits such as strawberries, raspberries or red currants.

SERVES 6–8
1¼ cups all-purpose flour
¼ cup cornstarch
1½ oz confectioners' sugar
8 tbsp butter
1 tsp vanilla extract
2 egg yolks, beaten
FILLING
7 oz cream cheese, softened
3 tbsp lemon curd
grated rind and juice of 1 lemon
confectioners' sugar, to sweeten
  (optional)
8 oz mixed red berry fruits
3 tbsp red currant jelly

1 Sift the flour, cornstarch and confectioners' sugar together, then rub in the butter until the mixture resembles bread crumbs.

2 Beat the vanilla into the egg yolks, then mix into the crumbs to make a firm dough, adding cold water if necessary.

3 Roll out and line a 9 in round pie pan, pressing the dough well up the sides after trimming. Prick the base of the tart with a fork and allow it to rest in the refrigerator for 30 minutes.

4 Preheat the oven to 400°F. Line the tart with waxed paper and baking beans. Place the pan on a baking sheet and bake for 20 minutes, removing the paper and beans for the last 5 minutes. When cooked, cool and remove the pastry shell from the pie pan.

VARIATION

There are all sorts of delightful variations to this recipe. For instance, leave out the red currant jelly and sprinkle lightly with confectioners' sugar or decorate with fresh mint leaves. Alternatively, top with sliced kiwi fruits.

5 Cream the cheese, lemon curd and lemon rind and juice, adding a little confectioners' sugar to sweeten, if you wish. Spread the mixture into the tart.

6 Top the tart with the fruits. Warm the red currant jelly and trickle it over the fruits just before serving.

Avocado and Lime Ice Cream

In some parts of the world, avocadoes are frequently eaten as desserts. In fact, their rich texture makes them perfect for a smooth, creamy and delicious ice cream.

SERVES 4–6
4 egg yolks
1¼ cups whipping cream
½ cup granulated sugar
2 ripe avocadoes
grated rind of 2 limes
juice of 1 lime
2 egg whites
few unsalted pistachio nuts, to serve

1 Beat the yolks in a heatproof bowl. In a saucepan, heat the cream with the sugar, stirring it well until it dissolves.

2 As the cream rises to the top of the pan at the point of boiling, remove it from the heat.

3 Gently pour the beaten egg yolks into the scalded cream, adding them in small amounts from a height above the saucepan. This stops the mixture from curdling. Allow the mixture to cool, stirring it occasionally, then chill.

COOK'S TIP

If you have an ice cream machine, then simply pour the mixture into the basin and switch on. No need to add the egg whites as air is already beaten in with the paddle.

4 Peel and mash the avocadoes until they are smooth then beat them into the custard with the lime rind and juice. Check for sweetness. Ice cream should be quite sweet before freezing as it loses flavor when ice cold. Add extra sugar now if you think it is needed.

5 Pour the mixture into a shallow container and freeze it until it is slushy. Beat it well once or twice as it freezes to stop large ice crystals forming.

6 Whisk the egg whites until softly stiff and fold into the ice cream. Return the mixture to the freezer and freeze until firm. Cover and label. Use within four weeks, decorated with pistachio nuts.

Honey and Lemon Spicy Mincemeat

Like Christmas Pudding, mincemeat is best made a few weeks ahead to allow the flavors to mature. This mixture is lighter than most traditional recipes.

MAKES 3 LB
1 cup vegetarian shredded suet
1½ cups currants
1 large cooking apple, coarsely grated
grated rind of 2 lemons
grated rind and juice of 1 orange
¾ cup no-need-to-soak prunes, chopped
¾ cup pitted dates, chopped
1 cup raisins
1¼ cups sultanas
1 cup flaked almonds
6 tbsp honey
4 tbsp brandy or rum
1 tsp cinnamon
½ tsp ground cloves or allspice

1 Mix all the ingredients together well in a large mixing bowl. Cover and store in a cool place for two days, stirring the mixture occasionally.

2 Sterilize clean jam jars by placing them in a warm oven for 30 minutes. Cool, then fill with mincemeat, and seal with wax discs and screw tops. Label and store until required.

Cinnamon and Molasses Cookies

The smell of home made cookies baking is bettered only by their wonderful taste! These cookies are slightly sticky, spicy and nutty.

MAKES 24
2 tbsp black molasses
4 tbsp butter or margarine
1 cup all-purpose flour
¼ tsp baking soda
½ tsp ground ginger
1 tsp ground cinnamon
¼ cup soft brown sugar
1 tbsp ground almonds or hazelnuts
1 egg yolk
1 cup confectioners' sugar, sifted

1 Heat the molasses and butter or margarine until they just begin to melt.

2 Sift the flour into a large bowl with the baking soda and spices, then stir in the sugar and almonds or nuts.

3 Beat the molasses mixture briskly into the bowl together with the egg yolk and draw the ingredients together to form a firm but soft dough.

4 Roll the dough out on a lightly floured surface to a ¼ in thickness and stamp out shapes, such as stars, hearts or circles. Re-roll the trimmings for more shapes. Place on a very lightly greased baking sheet and chill for 15 minutes.

5 Meanwhile, preheat the oven to 375°F. Prick the cookies lightly all over with a fork and bake them for 12–15 minutes until they are just firm. Cool on wire trays to crisp up.

6 To decorate, mix the confectioners' sugar with a little lukewarm water to make it slightly runny, then drizzle it over the cookies on the wire tray.

Mince Pies with Orange Cinnamon Pastry

Home made mince pies are so much nicer than store-bought, especially with a flavorsome pastry.

MAKES 18
2 cups all-purpose flour
1½ oz confectioners' sugar, plus a little extra for dusting
2 tsp ground cinnamon
10 tbsp butter
grated rind of 1 orange
4 tbsp ice cold water
1½ cups vegetarian mincemeat
1 beaten egg, to glaze

1 Sift together the flour, sugar and cinnamon, then rub in the butter until it forms crumbs. (This can be done in a food processor.) Stir in the grated orange rind.

2 Mix to a firm dough with the ice cold water. Knead lightly, then roll out to a ¼ in thickness.

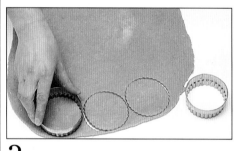

3 Using a 2½ in round cutter, cut out 18 circles, re-rolling as necessary. Then cut out 18 circles with a 2 in cutter. If liked, cut out little shapes from the centers of the smaller circles.

4 Line two muffin pans with the 18 larger circles – they will fill one and a half pans. Spoon a small spoonful of mincemeat into each pastry case and top with the smaller pastry circles, pressing the edges lightly together to seal.

5 Glaze the tops of the pies with egg and leave to rest in the refrigerator for approximately 30 minutes. Preheat the oven to 400°F.

6 Bake the pies for 15–20 minutes until they are golden brown. Remove them to wire racks to cool. Serve just warm and dusted with confectioners' sugar.

Christmas Pudding

If possible, try to make your puddings at least one month before Christmas for the flavors to develop and mature. Dried prunes and apricots add an unusual texture and delicious flavor to this recipe.

MAKES TWO 2 PINT PUDDINGS
5 cups fresh white bread crumbs
2 cups shredded vegetarian suet or ice cold butter, coarsely grated
1 cup all-purpose flour
1 cup soft brown sugar
2 tsp ground mixed spice
2½ cups currants
2½ cups raisins
1¾ cups sultanas
1 cup pitted no-need-to-soak prunes, chopped
¾ cup no-need-to-soak dried apricots, chopped
¾ cup candied citrus peel, chopped
¾ cup glacé cherries, washed and chopped
rind of 1 large lemon, grated
4 eggs, beaten
2 tbsp black molasses
⅔ cup beer or milk
4 tbsp brandy or rum

1 Grease two 2 pint Pyrex bowls and then line the base of each with small discs of waxed paper.

2 Mix all the ingredients together well. If you intend to put lucky coins or tokens in the mixture, boil them first to ensure they are clean and wrap them in foil.

3 Pack the mixture into the two bowls, pushing it down lightly.

4 Cover each pudding with greased waxed paper and a double thickness of foil. Secure the foil round the rim with lengths of kitchen string.

5 Place two old china saucers in the base of two large saucepans. Stand the basins on the saucers, pour boiling water to come two thirds of the way up and boil gently for about 6 hours, checking the water level regularly and topping it up with more boiling water.

6 When cooked, cool the puddings, remove the foil and paper then re-cover to store. On Christmas Day, re-boil for about 2 hours and serve with brandy butter and cream or custard.

Index

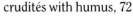